SAP® HANA Modeling
Practical World

Objectives of this book

SAP HANA has been widely adopted by the enterprises as an innovative platform to build high performance business analytics and related applications. As an in-memory database with massive parallel processing capabilities, HANA has opened up the possibilities to implement various solutions for analytics and enterprise applications with simplified processes and actionable insights. In this context, it becomes important to understand the key concepts and various best practices for implementing analytics using HANA modeling solutions.

The key objective of this book is to provide essential guidance to the HANA professionals and learners about the approaches and best practices to implement HANA modeling solutions, by sharing various project learnings, practical scenarios and tips. The topics presented in this book will provide essential concepts, examples, tips and solution approaches to build and maintain the HANA models for various use cases and requirements.

This book provides various insights on the overall HANA modeling process, which essentially involves the key activities such as requirement analysis for the KPIs, creating information models (views), implementing SQL Script based solutions, performance optimization of the models, performing testing and validations. It will help the readers who has basic HANA modeling skills, in understanding the practical application of various modeling features to achieve complex reporting requirements and to simplify the HANA modeling process.

Most importantly this book also covers few complex business cases for HANA models along with the detailed explanation of the solutions using the graphical calculation views and SQL script programming. This will greatly help the readers in understanding the practical application of the various HANA modeling artifacts and their features. In addition, the project learning and tips will help the readers in identifying and addressing some of the common issues in HANA modeling projects.

| SAP® HANA Modeling |
| Practical World |

Copyright © 2018   V S Narayana Varma Sree Vatsavayi

All rights reserved. No part of this publication may be reproduced, stored in a retrieval system, or transmitted in any form or by any means, without prior written, dated and signed permission of the author.

This publication contains references to the products of SAP SE or SAP AG. SAP, the SAP Logo, SAP HANA, SAP BW and other SAP Products and services mentioned herein are the registered trademarks of SAP SE or SAP AG. SAP assumes no responsibility for the content presented in this publication.

Disclaimer:

Although the author has made every effort to ensure that the information in this book was correct at press time, the author do not assume and hereby disclaim any liability to any party for any loss, damage, or disruption caused by errors or omissions, whether such errors or omissions result from negligence, accident, or any other cause.

The concepts, examples and screenshots of this book are mainly prepared based on SAP HANA Version 1 Support Pack 11 & 12. Hence the readers may find some differences in the content and screenshots depending on the specific HANA Database and HANA Studio versions that they use.

SAP® HANA Modeling
Practical World

Acknowledgements

I sincerely wish to thank TekLink leadership team, especially Mr. Pravin Gupta for all the support and encouragement, Mr. Sandeep Khare for his valuable guidance during the HANA projects, Mr. Amol Palekar, who is a well known author, for guiding me towards this publication process.

I would like to thank my friends and colleagues for all the positive influences, they have on me. I must thank my wife, my son, my parents and the rest of my family, who supported and encouraged me in spite of all the time it took me away from them. Above all, I would like to thank God for giving me all the strengh to accomplish this.

SAP® HANA Modeling
Practical World

TABLE OF CONTENTS

1   SAP HANA PLATFORM OVERVIEW AND USE CASES 1

   1.1   ARCHITECTURE AND BUILDING BLOCKS OF SAP HANA PLATFORM 2

   1.2   USE CASES AND SOLUTIONS ON SAP HANA PLATFORM 5

   1.3   SOLUTION APPROACH FOR HANA DATA MODELING PROJECTS 9

2   SAP HANA MODELING - DEVELOPEMENT STEPS 13

   2.1   ROLE OF SCHEMA AND PACKAGE IN HANA MODELING 13

   2.2   CREATING HANA MODELS USING THE DEVELOPER PERSPECTIVE 14

3   CALCULATION VIEWS - MODELING TECHNIQUES 26

   3.1   HOW TO DECIDE ON THE RIGHT TYPE OF HANA INFORMATION VIEW 26

   3.2   CALCULATION VIEWS – NODE TYPES 30

   3.3   CALCULATION VIEWS – ADDITIONAL BUILDING BLOCKS 46

   3.4   CALCULATION VIEW SEMANTICS 60

   3.5   BEST PRACTICES FOR IMPLEMENTING CALCULATION VIEWS 67

   3.6   CALCULATION VIEW EXAMPLES 70

4   SQL SCRIPT PROGRAMMING AND APPLICATIONS 108

   4.1   KEY ELEMENTS OF SQL SCRIPT PROGRAMMING 109

   4.2   TABLE FUNCTIONS 122

   4.3   STORED PROCEDURES 123

   4.4   PRACTICAL SOLUTIONS AND EXAMPLES USING SQL SCRIPT 127

5   HANA MODELING PRACTICAL CASE STUDIES 131

   5.1   BUSINESS CASE: BUILD CALCULATION VIEW FOR INVENTORY CYCLE COUNT 131

   5.2   BUSINESS CASE: SALES REVENUE PERCENTAGE SHARE CALCULATIONS 147

   5.3   BUSINESS CASE: REPORTING MONTH END INVENTORY BALANCES OF MATERIALS 152

   5.4   BUSINESS CASE: CALCULATING CUMULATIVE SALES REVENUES 163

SAP® HANA Modeling
Practical World

6 TESTING AND VALIDATION OF HANA MODELS **168**

   6.1   Effective validation techniques for SAP HANA Calculation Views.................... 168

   6.2   Preparing Test Plans for HANA Models 176

7 SMART TOOLS AND TECHNIQUES FOR PRODUCTIVITY **177**

   7.1   Tools and options to simplify the HANA modeling process 177

   7.2   Version Management of HANA Development Objects 181

   7.3   Tips for leveraging Built-in Tables in HANA 183

8 PERFORMANCE TUNING TECHNIQUES FOR HANA MODELS **186**

   8.1   Performance analysis tools in HANA 186

   8.2   Using Plan Visualizer Tool for Query Performance Analysis 187

   8.3   Explain Plan Functionality 191

   8.4   Tracing Tools for HANA Queries.. 193

   8.5   Calculation View – Performance Optimization Techniques............................ 198

9 TRANSPORTING HANA MODELS **199**

   9.1   Overview of Transport Mechanism for HANA data models 199

   9.2   Transporting HANA data models using Change Recording 201

1 SAP HANA Platform Overview and Use Cases

SAP HANA platform essentially provides the services related to database, application and integration to simplify and accelerate the traditional business applications and supports even modern business applications such as Internet of Things, Predictive analytics, Cloud and Big Data integration etc. These services are being constantly upgraded by SAP to address more business challenges and deliver range of solutions with greater speed and flexibility.

Key Features of SAP HANA Platform:

- In-Memory Appliance: Allows larger data volumes to be processed in real time

- Columnar Storage: Optimized for analytics and data retrieval and high level of compression leading to lesser storage footprint

- Parallel Processing: Multi-core achitecture and columnar storage provides parallel processing resulting in faster response times

- Open for integration: Variety of applications and tools can be integrated with SAP HANA using various standard methods such as SQL, MDX

In this context, it is essential for us to be aware of the variety of use cases that can be addressed based on SAP HANA platform and the various approaches that cans be adopted to deliver best possible solutions.

Background of Column Store and In-Memory Database:

In a columnar database, all values of a specific column (e.g. Customer Number) are stored consecutively at one location, resulting significantly faster access than traditional row-store oriented database. Columnar database will use compression techniques such as Dictionary encoding to store data efficiently. This   kind of storage and access mechanism enables much faster aggregation operations like Sum, Min, Max, Count and Average.

With SAP HANA, all data is stored in memory (RAM), which allows the processors (CPUs) to quickly access the data for processing. Typically SAP HANA can process around 1b scans/second/core and 10 m rows/second join performance. SAP HANA is basically an appliance with multi-core CPUs, multiple CPUs per board and multiple boards per server-all running in parallel provides enormous computational power.

1

1.1 Architecture and building blocks of SAP HANA Platform

SAP HANA is an in-memory computing based appliance which consists range of services related to data integration, database management, application development related to diverse set of fuctionalities such as analytics, text, graph, Big Data, Native applications etc.

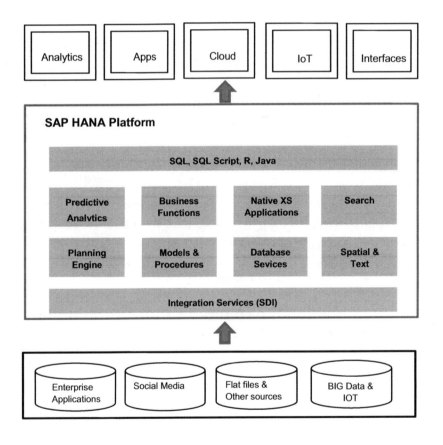

Key features of SAP HANA Database and Appliance

- Storing data in column store instead of the conventional row store
- Reducing the data foot print due to the compression techniques
- In-memory storage of the data allowing faster query response times
- Massive parallel processing due to the multi core architecture and the column engine capabilities
- Insert only approach in adding or changing records
- Cloud and On-premise support
- Multi Tenant database support to run more than one application on single HANA database

Typical request processing flow in SAP HANA database, when we run a query against any data model:

1. Request (query) is sent to the session manager, which in turn performs the authentication and opens the session connection
2. The query will be sent to the appropriate Request Processing service such as SQL, MDX or Calculation engine – which inturn uses the optimizer to prepare the execution plan and executes the query
3. Then the query will access all the relevant data from the column store where the tables are residing in the in-memory storage
4. Once the query execution is completed, results will be returned back to the Client application such as HANA studio or the Reporting client which are connected using ODBC or MDX

Architecture and components of SAP HANA Instance:

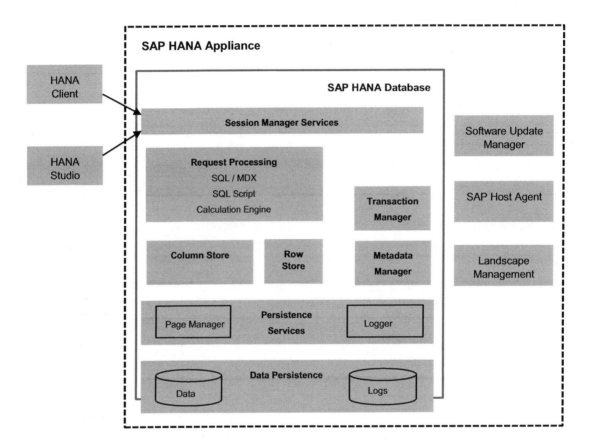

Tools for develeopers to access HANA database and build models and applications:

HANA Studio: It is an eclipse based desktop tool to perform data modeling, administration etc.

HANA Web IDE: It provides web based access to the HANA modeling, development and administration functions

1.2 Use Cases and Solutions on SAP HANA Platform

Let us understand the some of the common use cases where we can leverage the HANA platform and it's wide range of capabilites and services.

1.2.1 SAP HANA based Agile Data Marts

Data mart solutions are built to deliver a single source of KPI repository based on information views to provide real time reporting and ad-hoc analysis. HANA based data mart solutions are generally delivered as virtual data modesl (views) developmed as per the various KPI definitions of speicifc business processes.

Examples: Procurement analytics, Financial reporting data mart etc.

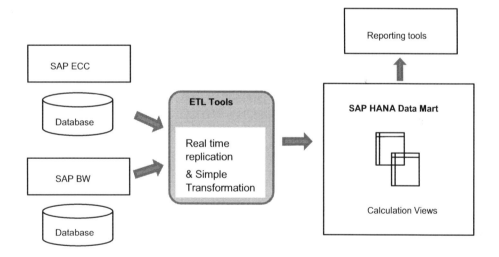

1.2.2 Enterprise Data Warehouse (EDW) solutions based on HANA

SAP HANA can be utilized as a platform to build standalone Data Warehousing Solution with the persistence of historical truth and reporting using virtual data models. However building an EDW solution based on HANA platform needs more efforts in the ETL logic since it does not have the built-in functionalities (Type 2 dimensional models such as Master data attributes, Multi dimesional models etc.) of a Data Warehouse solution like SAP BW.

To build HANA based EDW solution, we need to use the ETL tool to implement all the relevant transformations such as generating the delta records, key values for master data, merging data from multiple tables, storing historical snapshots etc. We need to build HANA views on these persisted tables. As a result, HANA EDW solutions are not generally meant for real time reporting.

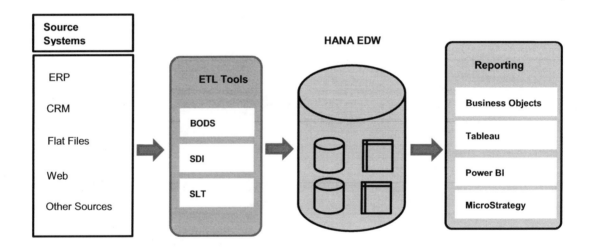

1.2.3 BW on HANA Mixed Scenaios

Implementing BW on HANA mixed scenarios to achieve greater flexibility and high performance in reporting along with the reduction in data footprint.

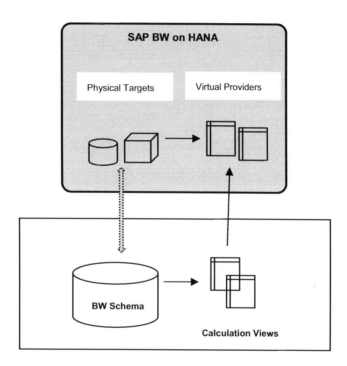

Key optimization areas related to HANA modeling in SAP BW on HANA
- Code push down for Transformations
- Optimized BW info providers based on HANA in-memory atrchitecure
- Flexibility of consuming HANA views in BW info providers

1.2.4 Business Solutions with complex rules and calculations

SAP HANA Platform can be chosen by the enterprises to address the requirements which involoves calculations that are highly memory and / or process intensive and involving manual operations. With the Code to Data approach of SAP HANA platform we will be able to build these solutions using the SQL Script and other standard programming functions such as APL, PAL, R.

- Complex calculations such as deriving Pricing buckets, Retail Point of Sales analytics which were highly cumbersome to generate using the traditional applications
- Planning applications (BW Integrated Planning) at more granular level (such as customer, product, calendar day) with closer visibility of latest estimates and trade spends, which was not possible with traditional databases. Planning functions can be implemented based on SQL Script, which helps in optimizing the performance drastically due to the code push dwon approach.
- Generating the results and calculations that are needed for external applications – For example generate a list of invoices that need to be sent to a third party on a weekly basis
- Custom business applications that needs solutions based on predictive analytics, big data etc.

Typical architecture for implementing complex calculations in SAP HANA:

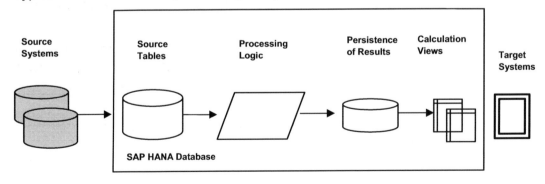

1.3 Solution Approach for HANA Data Modeling projects

Building analytics and data mart solutions using SAP HANA enterprise data modeling offers various benefits, compared to the traditional data warehousing solutions such as SAP BW. Knowing these benefits will help us to deliver the analytic reporting solutions which are agile, efficient, accurate and cost-effective, leading to greater customer satisfaction.

Key benefits of HANA data mart solutions:
- Virtual data models with on the fly calculation of Key Performance Indicators (KPIs) and reporting metrics, which enables reporting accuracy and requires very limited data storage – powered by the in-memory processing, columnar storage and parallel processing etc.

- Ability to perform highly processing intensive calculations efficiently – For example identify the customers where the sales revenue is greater than the average sales revenue per customer

- Flexible data models which caters to both the highly summarized reports and the detailed line item level reports

- HANA models can be easily consumed from variety of reporting tools, even helps us to meet self-service reporting needs

- Most importantly HANA data models are faster to implement and easier to apply any necessary changes as part of the maintenance and support, as there is generally one level of persistence for the data and all the necessary calculations are performed in different layers of HANA views.

- Reduced maintenance costs – Compared to the traditional data warehousing solutions where significant efforts are involved in monitoring the data loads, performing clean-up activities for administrative data, HANA requires very limited efforts in maintaining the data mart solution.

Apart from the HANA sidecar or data mart solutions, HANA modeling also plays an essential role in the BW on HANA mixed scenarios, S/4 HANA Analytics, Predictive Analytics and Native HANA applications etc.

SAP® HANA Modeling	SAP HANA Platform Overview and Use Cases
Practical World	

1.3.1 Starting steps: Requirement analysis

Understand the reporting requirements of the project clearly and try to conceptualize the HANA models to be built based the required KPIs. Few key aspects of the solution design: KPI definition including the details such as data sources, dimensions, filters, calculation logic, granularity and data volumes etc.

Below are some of the essential details to be clear and captured as part of the specifications for each of the KPIs requested by the business users:
1) Attributes to be included in the output- Level of granularity
2) Formula definition (i.e. the calculation logic)
3) Aggregation behavior (such as sum, average, maximum etc.)
4) User selections and filters to be enforced
5) Requirement for currency or unit conversions
6) Expected data latency – Real time or periodic such as weekly or monthly
7) Performance expectations

At times, the business users would expect HANA models to deliver best performance even with wide open selection criteria and with many columns in the output. Even though SAP HANA data models are expected to deliver sub-second response time, we need to be aware that there will be limited resources (memory, processing engines) in a HANA instance. Hence it is essential to communicate these aspects with the business users clearly and implement the HANA models to deliver optimal performance, by adopting the best practices and performance guidelines.

1.3.2 Implementation methodology: Waterfall vs Agile or Iterative

Traditionally most of the data warehousing projects are implemented using the waterfall methodology, which goes through various phases starting from the requirement analysis to final deployment and go-live followed by the project closure activities. While this model is effective for implementing solutions, which have clearly defined project objectives and specifications, the major drawback would be the lack of visibility of the solution to the end users until the completion of the project.

Hence it is recommended to adopt the agile or iterative implementation method for HANA data mart projects, as per which the overall solution is further divided into logical pieces (iterations) and these iterations will be implemented one after another, with some possible overlap. This method allows us to engage the business users throughout the lifecycle of a project in validating and obtaining feedback about the solution. This will help us to ensure that the final solution meets all the requirements as expected by the business users. In addition, this method will also help us in gathering the learnings from each iteration and utilizing the same in the remaining iterations.

In the iterative method each iteration will consists of various phases such as design, build, test and deploy. Accordingly, we need to plan the resource assignment for various activities like ETL development, HANA modeling, report development and security setup. During the project planning phase, identify the iterations to be implemented and the set of deliverables for each of the iteration.

Recommended approach for defining the iterations:

1) The first iteration can be planned to implement a simpler module, which also allows us to test the end to end solution – starting from ETL to reporting. This will help us in taking the early feedback from business users about the reporting templates, functionality and other semantics

2) Plan the next iterations based on the KPI priorities – i.e. implement the most critical data models and reports

3) Ideal to implement the "nice to have" type of data models and reports as part of final iteration

Below is an example to understand the iterative approach for HANA modeling projects.

Iteration 1 From – To Date	Iteration 2 From – To Date	Iteration 3 From – To Date
• Master data • Purchase order reporting	• Cash flow reports • Invoice reporting • Vendor performance dashboard	• Contract and agreements • Documentation and Knowledge Transfer
Build Test Cutover	Build Test Cutover	Build Test Cutover

1.3.3 Project team mix and essential skills

For successful execution of any project, having the right mix of skilled resources is essential. In the context of HANA data mart solutions, depending on the scope, ETL requirements and the reporting tools needed, following are the skills generally required.

- HANA Modelers with strong SQL and Database skills and preferably good experience in data modeling solutions (Data warehousing / OLAP reporting)

- ETL skills – BO Data services / SLT etc.

- Reporting skills in the respective tools such as Business objects, Tableau

- ABAP Programming skill will be essential in certain areas such as SLT, understanding the functionality in ECC, S/4HANA or BW solutions etc.

- Business domain skills and good understanding of SAP Business suite tables – This will be essential to understand the KPI requirements clearly and translate them into effective models

1.3.4 Test the waters before diving deep

Validate the features, tools and integration aspects:

Typically, HANA modeling projects will involve various tools and interfaces to deliver the end-to-end reporting solution. This includes the source systems, ETL tools and reporting tools etc. We need to configure the integration of these tools and applications to enable the communication with HANA database. Hence it is advisable to start with the prototype of a sample end-to-end solution, before proceeding with the full- fledged implementation.

The key steps in the prototyping of solution will be:

- Setting up data provisioning using Smart Data Integration (SDI), SLT, BODS

- Building HANA artifacts such as tables, information views, stored procedures etc.

- Consuming HANA views from the reporting tools

Prototyping will help us in verifying if all the functionalities are working as expected. With this approach we can validate the end-to-end data flow, right from the source system to the reporting client and address all the related issues beforehand. In this process, we need to engage the respective system administrators and security consultants to ensure all the appropriate software tools are installed, connections and integration points are established, security roles are maintained as per the requirements.

2 SAP HANA Modeling - Developement Steps

In this unit, let us understand the key components related to SAP HANA data modeling solutions and the process of building these components in a structured manner. In each of the HANA instance, the development artifacts are shown under the two folders namely "Catalog" and "Content".

Content folder represents the HANA repository and stores the design time version of the objects. All the HANA development artifacts of the repository content are organized under the packages to enable the transport. Once we activate a HANA development artifact corresponding runtime version is generated, which is stored under the catalog.

Catalog represents the actual metadata stored in HANA database, which consists of the runtime versions of all objects such as database tables, information views, stored procedures etc. Catalog objects are stored under the respective schemas.

2.1 Role of Schema and Package in HANA modeling

Schemas are used to logically organize the objects in a database. Which means any database object like a table, stored procedure or a view will be uniquely identified with <Schema Name>.<Object Name>

In HANA instance, schemas generally represent the source systems (ECC, BW, Flat file etc.) and there will be a schema created for each database user in HANA. In addition, there are pre-defined schemas such as _SYS_BIC (consists of all the generated modeling artifacts – calculation views, stored procedures etc.), _SYS_BI and SYS which contains the important system tables and views that stores the metadata information.

Packages: Are used to classify all the development objects in HANA repository. Packages can be nested as well. We need to define the appropriate package structure to classify the modeling content (views, tables, procedures etc.) as per the reporting hierarchy. Packages are also used to group the HANA development objects that are to be transported together. We need to assign the package to a Delivery unit to make the objects under the package as transportable.

As a best practice always adopt specific naming standards to define the package hierarchy. For example: ProjectOne.Finance.AP

2.2 Creating HANA models using the Developer Perspective

Understand the process of creating HANA development and modeling objects in the HANA repository:

This approach allows the developers to maintain objects in their local desktop and share with the team by updating to the repository. Apart from this, it will also provide the mechanism to transport all the development artifacts, since all the objects are created under packages in the developer perspective.

Especially the database artifacts such as column or row store tables, stored procedures are not transportable when they are created using the SQL statements such as CREATE COLUMN TABLE, CREATE PROCEDURE, since they are not maintained under packages. Hence the best approach for creating such database objects is to use the Development Perspective (hdbtable / hdbprocedure syntax), which is explained in the following sections.

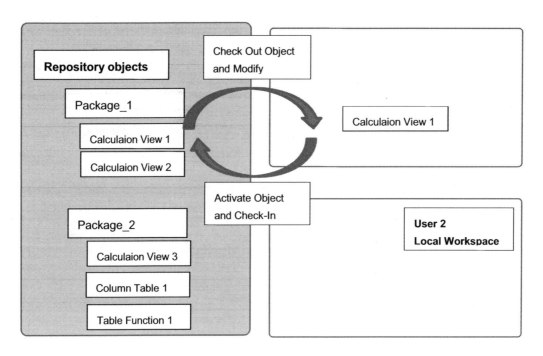

Repository: Stores all the HANA development artifacts centrally in the HANA Database instance.

Workspace: Allows us to import the development artifacts into our local machine and make the necessary changes, then export them back to the repository

Below are the detailed steps and explanations to understand the methods of utilizing the development perspective:

2.2.1 Working with the HANA Development Perspective:

Systems Tab
Step 1: Create a Package
Package: It groups all the information models and makes it easier to transport (import/export) them across difference systems in the HANA Landscape

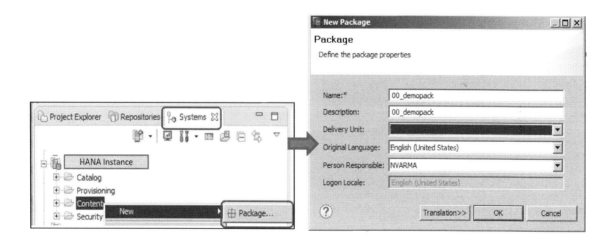

Repositories Tab:
Step 2: Create Workspace

Repository workspace: is the location for all development files that supports version control when sharing between developers. Each repository workspace will be assigned to a folder in the User's local machine, where the development artifacts can be edited.

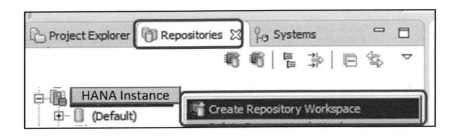

Enter the workspace properties and save

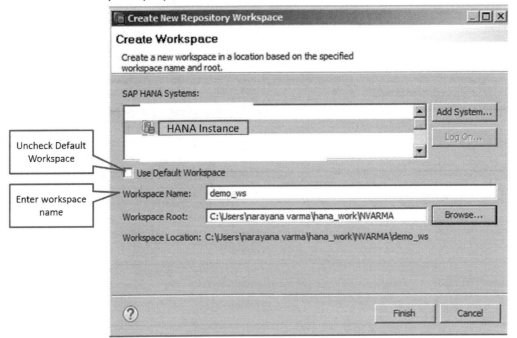

Observe the local folder generated in your system.

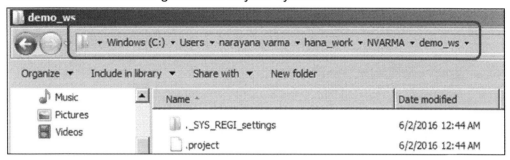

Project Explorer Tab:

Step 3: Create a Project

Projects group together all application-related artifacts, containing folders and files for the application. Multiple projects can be placed into one repository workspace.

Note: Projects are mainly essential while building native applications in SAP HANA platform. To build HANA modeling related artifacts, it is optional step to create projects.

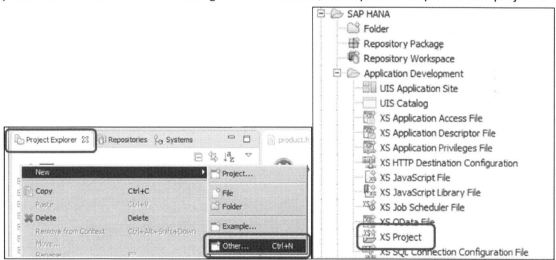

Note: Deselect the checkbox "Share project in SAP repository" if you want to maintain the development artifacts in a different folder before sharing with the repository workspace folder

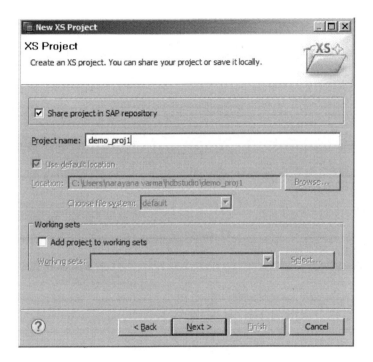

Choose the workspace, which is to be associated with the project location and the select the package, in which the development artifacts have to be created or changed.

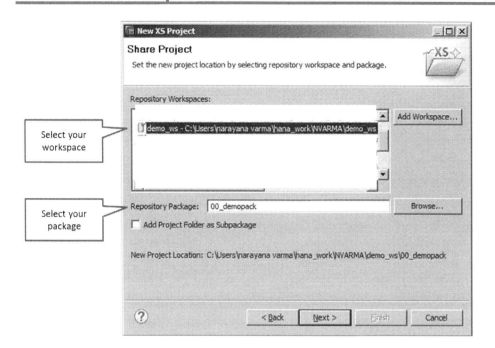

Optionally we can choose the Schema to be created.

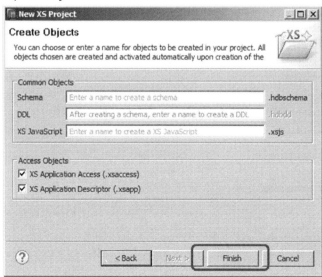

Save the Project.

2.2.2 Building Repository Objects in HANA Development Perspective

Implementing Database objects using HDB Table Syntax:

Switch to the Repository tab:

Right click on the package : Choose New → Other..

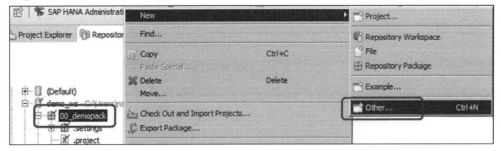

Select "Database table"

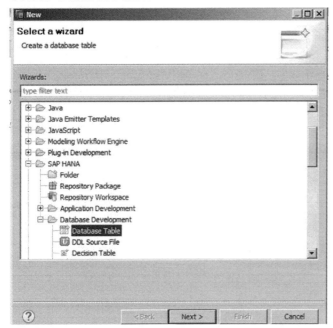

Enter the file name which represent the database table.

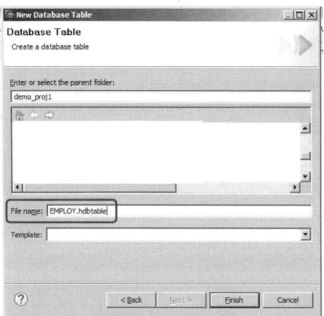

Note: We can also choose the available "Template" in the above window to get the sample definition and coding of the object.

Enter the table definition in the editor:

```
table.schemaName = "NVARMA";
table.tableType = COLUMNSTORE;
table.columns = [
 {name = "EMP_ID"; sqlType = NVARCHAR; length = 10;},
 {name = "EMP_NAME"; sqlType = NVARCHAR; length = 40;}] ;

table.primaryKey.pkcolumns = ["EMP_ID"];
```

Save and **Activate** the table definition.

Observe the fully qualified name of the table, which follows the convention:

<Schema>.<package path >/<Object name>

2.2.3 Essential Database objects in HANA:

Database Object	Extension	Usage
Database Table	.hdbtable	Persistence of data
DDL Source file	.hdbdd	To define data types for reusability
Scalar Function	.hdbscalarfunction	Reusable functions that returns single value
Table Function	.hdbtablefunction	Reusable functions that returns data in table structure
Schema	.hdbschema	Schemas are used to group database objects
Structure	.hdbstructure	To define reusable structure data types
Stored Procedure	.hdbprocedure	To implement reusable routines

2.2.4 Important options to maintain HANA development objects

Let us understand the importance and usage of the different options available in the HANA Development Perspective to maintain the HANA development artifacts. We can right click on a development artifact like calculation view, database table and perform the desired action from the popup menu.

Options in Repository tab:

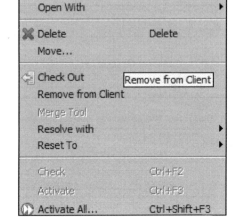

- *Check Out*: This option is used to bring the development object to the local workspace folder, whenever we need to implement any changes. We can perform this at the package level also to bring all the objects under the package to the local workspace

  Note: Multiple developers can perform the Check out on a specific object parallelly to edit the local version of the object.

- *Remove from Client*: This option is meant for the reversal of "Check out", which means it will remove the development object from the local workspace folder.

  Note: To ensure that you will be editing the latest version of the object from repository, it is recommended to perform "Remove from Client" on the object and perform the "Check Out" again.

- *Resolve with Local / Remote*: This option is used to resolve the conflicts with the merge process.

- *Reset to Active*: In certain situations, we may not wish to activate the changes to our object and we want to bring it back to its previous active state. Use this option in such cases to cancel the changes to a development object and bring it back to the recent active version.

- *Activate:* Use this option to activate the changes to the development artifact and commit the changes to the repository.

- *Delete:* Delete the object from repository

Note: The examples presented in this book are based on the respective schemas and packages in the specific HANA instance where these are implemented.

Example: `"NVARMA"."00_dmm::TF_SALES_CUMM_MONTHS" ( )`

NVARMA → Schema name

00_dmm → Package name

TF_SALES_CUMM_MONTHS → Object name

Accordingly, the readers need to implement the models using appropriate schema and packages within the HANA instance

2.2.5 HANA Studio – Quick View Functions and Modeler Perspective

While it is recommended to use the HANA Development Perspective for all the content development, in few cases we need to work in the Modeler perspective. Following are the key functions provided under the Quick View tool of Modeler perspective.

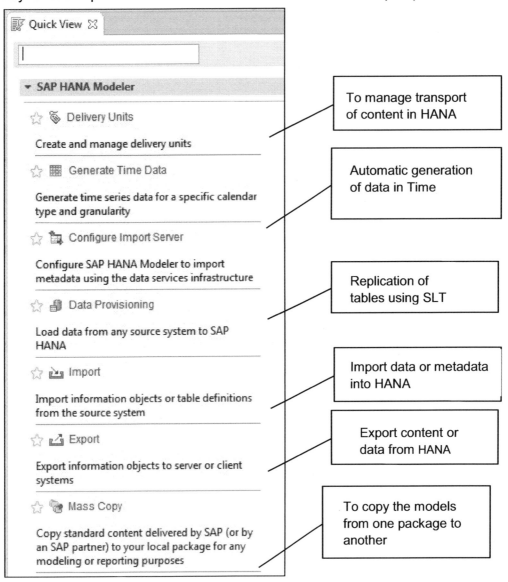

Quick View tool options continued...

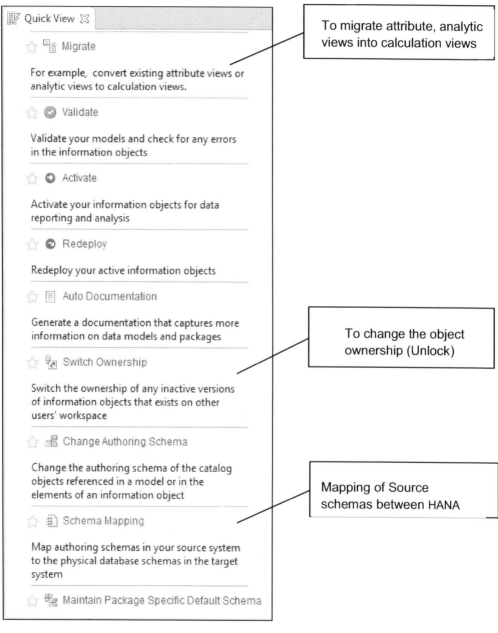

3 Calculation Views - Modeling Techniques

Overview of SAP HANA Modeling – Information Views

Implementing analytics and data mart solutions using HANA modeling largely involves the creation of different type of information views (Attribute, Analytical and Calculation views). The key differentiating factor between the traditional data warehousing solutions and HANA is, we will be implementing the entire logic virtually using various nodes in different layers. It also requires innovative thinking along with solid data modeling skills and a very good understanding of different SQL statements to build complex and effective HANA views.

In the recent releases like SP 10 and SP 11, HANA Modeling functionality has been greatly enriched with several new features to address various complex KPI requirements. All the graphical views must be implemented as Calculation views, since they were re-designed by SAP to replace the functionality of attribute and analytic views. As a best practice, it is always recommended to implement the models using graphical calculation views unless there are specific requirements that can be only implementing using SQL Script.

3.1 How to decide on the right type of HANA information view

While creating graphical calculation views, we need to implement the entire logic virtually using various nodes in different layers. It requires innovative thinking along with solid data modeling skills and a very good understanding of different SQL statements to build complex and effective HANA views.

Note: Always try to implement your HANA modeling solutions as per the features supported by the current support pack / revision level and consider the guidelines and future road-map of SAP.

- **Dimension** type calculation views: To model master data dimensions or to implement "value help" views for providing input values for selection prompts.
  Dimension type calculation views:

SAP® HANA Modeling Practical World — Calculation Views - Modeling Techniques

- Can only have attributes and no measures, since it does not support aggregations on data
- Not visible to the reporting tools. We can only consume these views in other modeling artifacts.
- Supports reusable hierarchy definitions
- Are the replacement of attribute views (From HANA 1.0 SPS 11)
- The default top level node for these views is a "Projection"

Example: Dimension Type Calculation view:

- **Cube type** calculation views: These are calculation views mainly built for the reporting. They include measures along with aggregation capabilities. We can consume all the other types of views inside the cube type calculation views

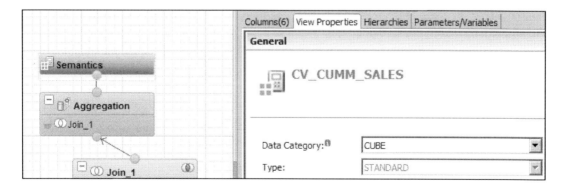

- **Star join** type calculation views: To build multidimensional view with star join functionality. They serve as an alternative to analytic views.

- **Table Functions**: These are implemented using SQL Script programming mainly to build solutions which cannot be accomplished using the Graphical views. Table functions are ideal choice for building reusable solutions which needs complex logic such as looping over result sets, performing complex look up operations etc.

Typical Data Modeling Flow in HANA

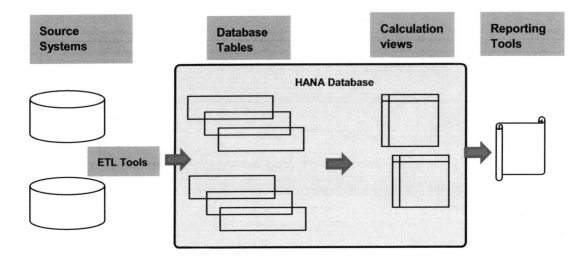

The above diagram illustrates the typical flow of data from the source systems to the reporting tools, in HANA based data mart or EDW solutions.

Data Provisioning methods (ETL Tools) for HANA: Quick Summary
- SLT (System Landscape Transformation) – Real time replication of tables using database level trigger- based approach from SAP or Non-SAP systems
- BO Data Services – Batch Oriented data provisioning with full-fledged ETL capabilities
- SDA (Smart Data Access) – Accessing data from remote database
- SDI (Smart Data Integration) – Native HANA tool to address the common ETL features including real time replication, transformations, remote database access etc.

3.1.1 Key features of Graphical Calculation Views

Graphical calculation views are the preferred choice because of the following reasons:

✓ **Optimal performance** (column pruning, filter pushdown ability etc.)

Column Pruning: Whenever we run a query on a calculation view, the optimizer will only process the columns which are requested in the query, even though the calculation view has many other columns exposed in the output. This will result in superior performance in HANA column engine.

Filter Pushdown: The volume of data which is to be processed by the query on a calculation view can be minimized by enforcing necessary filters on various columns. These filters are pushed down to the database table access level, leading to the optimal query performance.

✓ **Ease of maintenance** (easy to understand the model and apply required changes): It would be simple to implement changes to the calculation views, such as adding new attributes, measures, calculated columns or changing the formulas etc.

✓ **Simple to validate** There are multiple tools and options to validate the data in calculation views. Mainly we can use the data preview and debugging features to verify the results at individual node level.

✓ **Supports modular approach to build the KPIs** – we can build calculation views in multiple layers for reusability

However graphical calculation views do not allow us to implement certain complex business logic such as recursive operations and certain complex lookup operations. In those scenarios we are supposed to build the solutions using SQL Script based artifacts such as the stored procedures and table functions. These concepts are covered in the later units.

3.1.2 Different Types of Data Sources for Graphical Calculation Views

One of the primary building blocks of calculation views is the data sources from where the data is retrieved into the model.

Following are the different types of data sources that can be used while implementing calculation views.

- Database tables
- Database Views
- Calculation Views, Analytic Views and Attribute Views
- Virtual Tables (based on Smart Data Access) – used for remote data access
- Table Functions (Replaces Scripted Calculation Views)

3.2 Calculation Views – Node Types

Let us understand some of the essential tips and techniques in HANA modeling, to understand the various types of modeling artifacts, their features and functionalities and how to apply them to meet the overall KPI requirements.

Graphical calculation views are made of the following building blocks, which are generically called as "Nodes". Understanding the configuration, functionality and limitations for each of these node types plays an important role to build effective solutions for the various kind of reporting needs.

Each node in a calculation view corresponds to an SQL statement with a specific functionality such as merging records, summarizing records and filtering records.

SAP® HANA Modeling Practical World | Calculation Views - Modeling Techniques

3.2.1 Projection node functionality

Projection nodes are widely used in graphical calculation views to optimize the performance because of these stated functionalities.

Projection node will allow us to:
- Fetch the subset of columns from a data source
- Apply the filter conditions to fetch only relevant rows in the output

Because of these two features, we can achieve optimized performance using projection nodes in calculation views.

Example: To get specific fields of Sales Document Header (VBAK Table) with the filter criteria on Sales Document Type (VBTYP = C for Sales Orders) and Created Date (ERDAT)

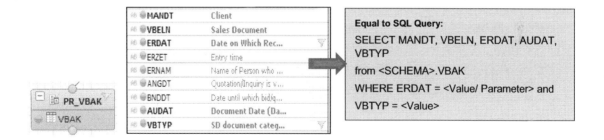

Note: Projection node will not perform any grouping or of records.

3.2.2 Aggregation node - Usage scenarios

Aggregation node is primarily meant for grouping and summarizing the source records. It can be used to address multiple scenarios while implementing calculation views.

- Summarizing the measures based on group of attribute columns, using variety of aggregation options (Count, Sum, Maximum, Minimum, Average, Standard Deviation)
- Look up operation of specific data set and perform calculations, such as determine last modified date for each sales document.
- Fetch distinct set of records based for a specific combination of attributes

Key points about aggregation node:

- We can also apply the filters on attributes or measures at an aggregation node.
- It is optional to have measures in an Aggregation node. An aggregation node without any measures is basically used to derive the distinct set of records for the set of attributes.
- Calculations or formulas implemented at an aggregation node are executed as "Calculation after aggregation"
- Aggregation on larger volume of records can be inefficient from performance point of view. Try to filter the data records as much as possible to ensure optimal performance.
- Use Projection node instead of Aggregation node, whenever there is no need for the grouping of records (deriving distinct values). This will help in improving the performance.
- Keep Flag on specific attributes: Use this to enforce "Calculation before aggregation". We need to set the Keep Flag property to "True" for those attributes, which are supposed to be always included in the query.

Let us look at the use cases related to each of the scenario for using aggregation node below

SAP® HANA Modeling Practical World — Calculation Views - Modeling Techniques

Aggregation Node Use Case #1: Summarizing the measures

To derive the SUM of Net Value (NETWR) for sales orders at Customer(KUNNR), Sales Organization(VKORG) and Month(CALMONTH) and Currency(WAERK) level

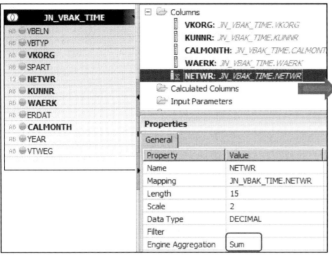

Results of the query on table VBAK:

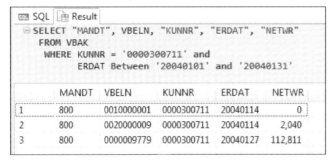

Results of the Aggregation Node:

VKORG	KUNNR	WAERK	CALMONTH	NETWR
3000	0000300711	USD	200401	114,851
3000	0000300712	USD	200401	40,955
3000	0000300715	USD	200401	38,850
3000	0000300717	USD	200401	45,500
3000	0000300719	USD	200401	497,401

Note: For the customer **0000300711** the value of NETWR is matching between the query on the source table and the Aggregation node.

Aggregation Node Use Case #2: Complex Look up operation and calculations

To get the Net Value of Latest Sales Order (Based on Sales Oder Date) for each Sold To Customer (Source table VBAK)

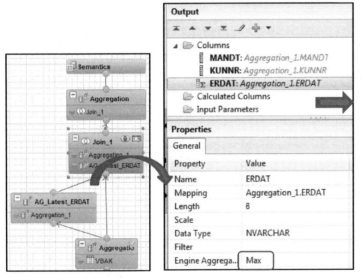

Results of Calculation View:

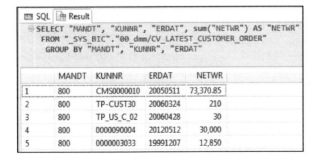

34

Results of SQL query on table

```
SELECT A.KUNNR, SUM(A.NETWR), A.ERDAT
  from VBAK as A
  INNER JOIN
      (SELECT MANDT, KUNNR, MAX(ERDAT) as LATEST_ERDAT from VBAK
          GROUP BY MANDT,KUNNR ) as B
  ON  A.MANDT = B.MANDT and
      A.KUNNR = B.KUNNR
      And A.ERDAT = B.LATEST_ERDAT
  WHERE A.MANDT = 800 and A.VKORG = '3000'
  GROUP BY A.MANDT,A.KUNNR, A.ERDAT
```

	KUNNR	SUM(NETWR)	ERDAT
1	CMS0000010	73,370.85	20050511
2	TP-CUST30	210	20060324
3	TP_US_C_02	30	20060428
4	CMS0000041	36,859	20120301
5	RFID_CUST	0	20110810

Aggregation Node Use Case #3: Derive distinct set of records for a combination of attributes

Fetch the distinct set of Materials from the list of Material / Plant combination records.

In the below example, we are using an aggregation node to bring only specific attributes (MATERIAL & PLANT) from the source projection node. There are no measures in this case. This aggregation node will derive the distinct set of Material / Plants as the result set.

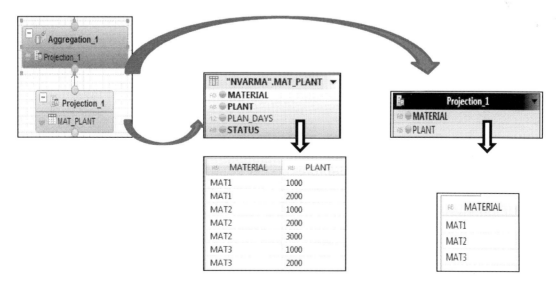

35

3.2.3 Important aspects of Joins

Joins are the most common type of nodes that we need to use while building calculation views, since they allow us to combine the results from two different sources based on a join criterion.

Always ensure that the right type of join has been implemented, since each of the join type has a specific behavior both from functionality and performance point of view. The first criteria to choose a join type is the required functionality and the second criteria is the performance of the join.

- **Inner joins** are preferred only when we must fetch the matching records from both the sources. From performance point of view, the basic disadvantage with inner joins is that it is always executed when we query the view. That means inner join is always processed even if the fields of both the sources are not used in the query.

- **Left outer joins** are preferred mostly, since they allow us to fetch the records even without the matching records from the right table. Another key advantage is, left outer joins are only processed when any of the fields from the right table are requested in the query. If no fields are requested from the right table, it will process the query as a single table access.

- **Referential joins** will function like inner join in the attribute views, where as in analytic views these are applied like left outer join. In Calculation views we can use Referential joins,

- **Full outer joins** are useful to bring the data records from both sides, even if there are no matching entries in either side of the join.

- **Text joins** are meant to display the language specific descriptions and are always executed like inner joins. Hence, the query will exclude data records for which the texts are not maintained.

- **Temporal Joins** are supported in Calculation view of type Star Join. These are used to derived time-dependent attributes for any specific dimension.

Key points about Join node:
- Ensure that the join condition includes all the relevant columns. Otherwise this will lead to duplication of records (because of the Cartesian product).
- The default Join type in a calculation view is "Inner Join". Hence, we need to ensure to change this to appropriate type of join as per the required functionality.

Join Node Use Case #1: Matching entries by enforcing referential integrity

To fetch only matching entries from Sales order header (VBAK) and the Time Dimension table. Since there is a filter applied on the Time Dimension (DATE_SQL), this join will ensure that only the Sales Order of the given DATE_SQL are fetched by join the operation.

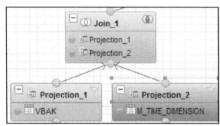

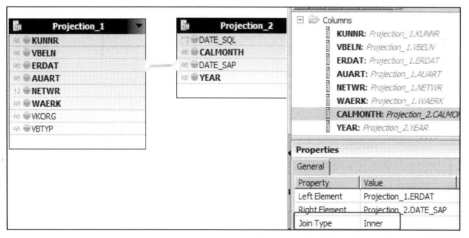

Like this example, we shall use inner joins to fetch only relevant data from transactional tables, which will ensure the data accuracy and results in optimal performance. At the same time, we should not choose inner join, when we are not supposed to bring only matching entries. Otherwise it will cause lead to a situation of missing relevant records in the result set.

Join Node Use Case #2: Look-up operations using Outer joins

In various scenarios, we need to perform a look-up on a dataset for the existence of a matching attribute or measure. Left outer joins are commonly used to achieve this.

In the below example, we are trying the derive the partner (Sales Rep) for each of the Sales orders. Even if there is no matching entry in VBPA table, it should still include the Sales order in the result set.

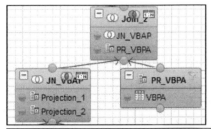

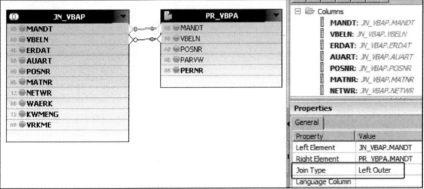

Join Node Use Case #3: Comparison operations using Full Outer joins

We have a requirement to derive the "Lifecycle Status" for each of the Materials based on Previous year and Current Year Sales orders.

- Materials with Sales orders in the both Previous and Current years: 'Active'
- Materials with Sales orders only in Current year: 'New'
- Materials with Sales orders only in Previous year: 'Inactive'

If we consider the Sales orders of Previous year as one dataset and the Sales orders of Current year as another dataset, using Full outer join we are going to get the records from both the data sets even if there is no matching record (Material) in either side.

SAP® HANA Modeling Practical World — Calculation Views - Modeling Techniques

Calculation view design: Using Full Outer Join

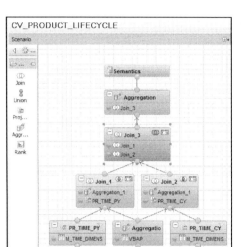
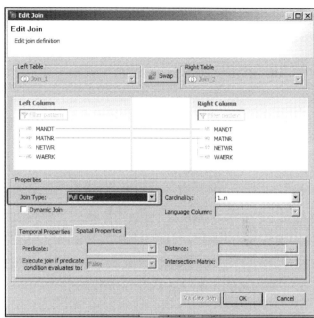

Preview the results of view: Observe the Lifecycle Status

MATNR_PY	MATNR_CY	LIFECYCLE_STATUS	NETWR_PY	NETWR_CY
SP CONSULTING PROJ	SP CONSULTING PROJ	Active	38,439,000	10,010,000
?	000000000000002000	New	?	0
?	GBT-FINISH1	New	?	110
?	100-100	New	?	20,000
?	HT-1055	New	?	105.3
?	PC_SERVICE_A	New	?	1,200
?	SER_021_ERP	New	?	500,811.24
?	SRV1_4_ERP	New	?	2,849.57
?	R-1150	New	?	15
?	SM-REPHOUR	New	?	32.78
?	JF-REPAIR	New	?	600
?	CM_CU_CONC	New	?	0
000000000000001800	?	Inactive	100,000	?
GTS-KMAT-01	?	Inactive	3,000	?
000000000000001837	?	Inactive	73.8	?

3.2.4 Union node usage criteria and techniques

Union node is used to merge the records from multiple sources, especially when these sources are having most of the dimensions (attributes) as common. Union operations are executed faster, since the records from all the sources are simply appended to the target result set and there is no need to compare the records based on some criteria, which is performed in join operations.

Key points about UNION node:
- Always prefer to use union over join, when the dimensions of source nodes are mostly common
- For each of the attribute and measure in the Union node output we need to ensure the mappings are correctly maintained from the respective source nodes.
    - If we do not map the attribute from all the sources, it will be considered as Null (?) and it leads to additional rows in the result set.
    - If we do not map the measure from any of the source, it will consider the value to be 0 from that source.
- Union node does not perform the aggregation of results, we need to use additional aggregation node to achieve this.
- We can implement calculated columns at a Union level.
- We cannot apply filters at Union node level. We need to use additional projection node on the Union node, to apply any filters
- Union node enables parallel processing- each of the data sources of union node will be executed independently and the results are merged together. This will certainly help in performance optimization
- We can create additional columns in the Union node output, which are primarily used to implement the "Constant Column" based solutions in calculation views (For example create an additional column called SOURCE_REGION that stores the constant values like 'US', 'EU'). Constant columns will allow us to address the records of specific source.

Union Node Use Case #1: Merging records from multiple sources of identical structure

Example: Actual vs Plan data sets, Data records from multiple regions etc.

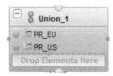

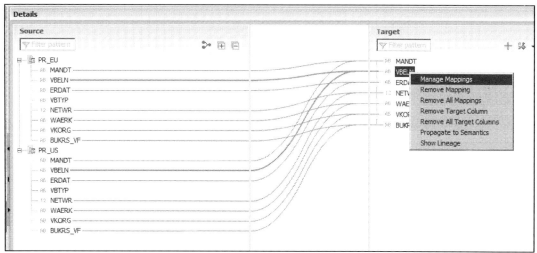

Sample result:

BUKRS_VF	WAERK	NETWR_SUM
0001	EUR	5,624,070
0001	USD	3,000
0005	EUR	1,140,000
1000	DEM	481,354,419.44
1000	EUR	695,634,486.12
1000	USD	52,308,828.1

Union Node Use Case #2: Common dimensions with different set of measures

Example: We have Plant and Material as common dimensions and each of the source node has specific measures:

Source Node1: YTD Sales, MTD Sales

Source Node1: No of Open Orders, No of Late Deliveries

In this case we can use Union node to draw these measures from multiple sources for a specific combination of attributes.

Union Node Use Case #3: Parallel operations and node level pruning

Union Node Pruning in calculation view helps us in improving the performance of the view by executing only specific source of the union operation based on the user input for specific attributes during the query runtime. This feature is available from HANA 1.0 SP11.

For example, if the union node is combining the results of 4 different regions such as NA (North America), LA (Latin America), EMEA (Europe and Middle east) and APAC (Asia Pacific). When we configure Union pruning for the calculation view, it will only run the query on the specific source based on user input. For example, if the user enters the company code related to the region NA, then only the source node related to NA will be processed during the query execution. For this we need to maintain the details in a Union Pruning configuration table.

Definition of Union Pruning Configuration Table: "NVARMA".00_dmm::UNION_PRUNE_CONFIG

```
table.schemaName = "NVARMA";
table.tableType = COLUMNSTORE;
table.columns =
  [
    {name = "SCHEMA";  sqlType = VARCHAR;  length = 30;  },
    {name = "CALC_SCENARIO";  sqlType = VARCHAR;  length = 120;  },
    {name = "INPUT";  sqlType = VARCHAR;  length = 200;  },
    {name = "COLUMN";  sqlType = VARCHAR;  length = 50;  },
    {name = "OPTION";  sqlType = VARCHAR;  length = 20;  },
    {name = "LOW_VALUE";  sqlType = VARCHAR;  length = 40;  },
    {name = "HIGH_VALUE";  sqlType = VARCHAR;  length = 40;  }
  ];
```

Maintain the following entries in the Pruning configuration table:

```
SQL   Result
    select * from NVARMA."00_dmm::UNION_PRUNE_CONFIG"
```

	SCHEMA	CALC_SCENARIO	INPUT	COLUMN	OPTION	LOW_VALUE	HIGH_VALUE
1	_SYS_BIC	00_dmm/CV_REGION_SALES	PR_US	BUKRS_VF	=	3000	
2	_SYS_BIC	00_dmm/CV_REGION_SALES	PR_US	BUKRS_VF	=	3050	
3	_SYS_BIC	00_dmm/CV_REGION_SALES	PR_EU	BUKRS_VF	=	1000	
4	_SYS_BIC	00_dmm/CV_REGION_SALES	PR_EU	BUKRS_VF	=	2000	

Layout of the calculation view below:

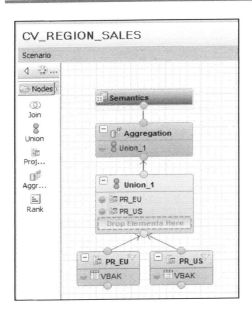

In the Calculation view propertes, choose the the "Pruning Configuration Table"

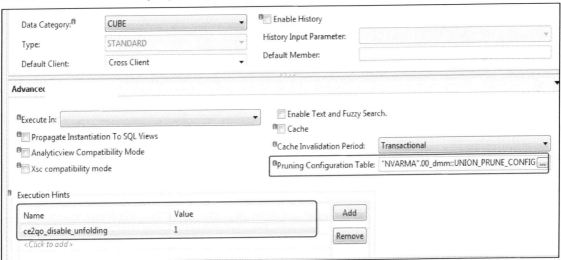

Note: Maintain the above mentioned Execution Hint. This will ensure that the union pruning is performed when we execute queries on this view.

Note: To be able to perform the Union Pruning the query engine expects the SQL query to have the numerical constants enclosed within single quotes:

Sample query on the calculation view:

	MANDT	VBELN	ERDAT	WAERK	VKORG	BUKRS_VF	NETWR
1	800	0005002304	20120711	GBP	2000	2000	0
2	800	0005002363	20120726	GBP	2000	2000	0
3	800	0005002367	20120726	GBP	2000	2000	0

Result: The query optimizer will process the node PR_EU only, since the company code belongs to this node as per the Union Pruning configuration table. This will lead to optimal performance of the calculation views. (Refer to the Plan Visualizer Example: Calculation view with Union Pruning - Unit 8 Section 8.4.3)

3.2.5 Leveraging Rank Node for deriving ordered result set

Rank node is used to derive Top N / Bottom N set of records from the data source, which helps us in producing the rankings.

Key elements in the definition of Rank Node:
- Sort Direction – Order of sorting to produce the rankings - Descending/Ascending.
- Threshold: This is the value for N, i.e., Rank Number/Top Number. It can be given directly as a fixed integer value or can be passed at run time using an input parameter.
- Order By: The columns based on which the sort must be performed. Here the column is typically a measure.
- Partition By – The column(s) based on which the sorting need to be applied

SAP® HANA Modeling Practical World — Calculation Views - Modeling Techniques

Rank Node Use Case: Generate ranking on result set based on specific measure

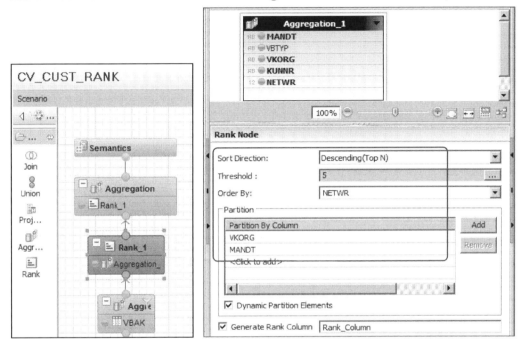

Preview the results and observe the new column "Rank_Column"

MANDT	VKORG	KUNNR	NETWR	Rank_Column
800	Z100	0000090051	10,545,866.29	1
800	Z100	0000090005	2,660,000	2
800	Z100	0000090040	1,497,012	3
800	Z100	0000090062	1,329,680	4
800	Z100	0000090064	846,160	5

Key points about RANK node:

- Rank node is executed by Row Store engine, which makes it very inefficient from performance point of view, especially when we apply it on larger result sets.

3.3 Calculation Views – Additional Building Blocks

Let us explore the other key features that helps us to implement calculation views with various additional functionalities.

3.3.1 Input Parameters and Variables

In various scenarios, we need to perform the operations such as calculations, filters, currency conversions based on the run time values which or either entered by users or derived dynamically.

Variables and Input parameters are meant to achieve this functionality in HANA views. Let us understand the key functionality and application of both these features.

Variables – These are used to apply restriction of records based on specific attribute values. We cannot address or reuse the variables anywhere in the calculation view such as in formulas etc. They are basically used to restrict the data records using the WHERE clause on specific attribute of the view.

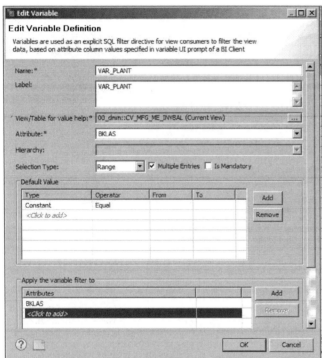

Note:

The above variable will be shown in the user prompt while running the data preview.

The values entered in the variable will be added to the query as WHERE BKLAS = '<Value>'

Input Parameters – These are used to pass values to the calculation views during runtime to perform various operations such as filtering, calculations, currency conversion etc. Due to their diverse functionality, input parameters are very useful in modeling calculation views.

We can use Input parameters to generate the necessary fields during the run time of a calculation view. There are various scenarios where input parameters are supported as Place Holders in the calculation view definition.

1) Filter expressions
2) Calculated column formulas
3) Currency / Unit conversions (Such as Target currency, Conversion Date etc..)
4) Rank node – to specify the number of rankings

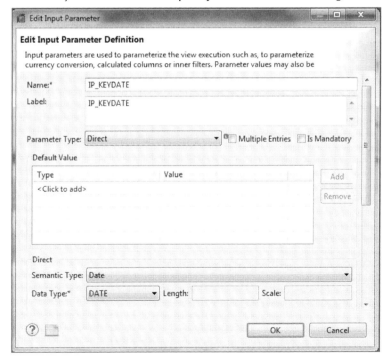

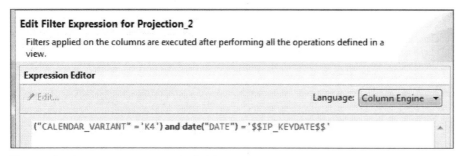

Example: Input parameter definition and usage in the filter expression of Projection node.

Input Parameter Types: Controls the process of deriving the value at runtime

- Direct / Column (via User input or Default value)

    This method is used to provide the value via user input or default value based on constant or expression.

- Static List

    With this option, we can present a list of values to the user to choose from.

- Derived from Table

    Using this option, we can read the values from specific record of a database table by providing necessary filter criteria.

- Derived from Stored Procedure or Scalar Function

    Using this option, we can read the values from specific record of a database table by providing necessary filter criteria.

Input Parameters for data exchange between the Models:

Another important usage of the Input parameters is the ability to transfer the data between different modeling objects. Using the "Manage mappings" option we can achieve this in a calculation view.

- Data Sources: To map the input parameters between calculation views in a stacked model
- Views for Value Help: To pass the values to Value help views
- Procedures / Scalar functions: To pass the values to stored procedures or scalar functions which are used to derive the values for other input parameters

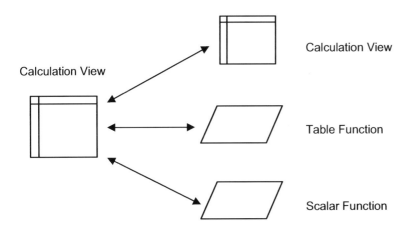

Example: Manage Mappings for Input Parameters

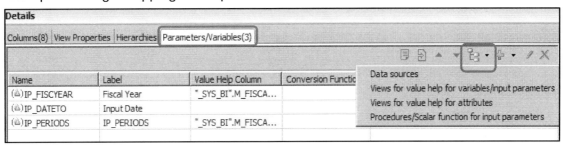

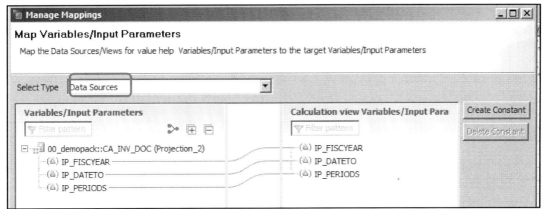

Note: We can also pass Constant values to the input parameters using the "Create Constant" option above.

3.3.2 Calculated Columns and Formulas – Essential tips

Calculated columns allow us to implement additional measures and attributes as per the KPI definitions and requirements.

- We can implement calculated columns at the Projection, Aggregation, Union and Join S
- The formulas for calculated columns can be implemented based on Column Engine or SQL Engine. Since both these variants run on the different engines, accordingly the syntax and supported expression and functions will be different.

Calculated Columns based on Column Engine:

Provides various built-in functions related to: Data type conversions, String and Date operations, mathematical functions, conditional operation such as IF, IsNull etc.

Calculated Columns based on SQL Engine:

Provides various built-in functions supported by the SQL engine: Data type conversions, String and Date operations, mathematical functions.

Example:

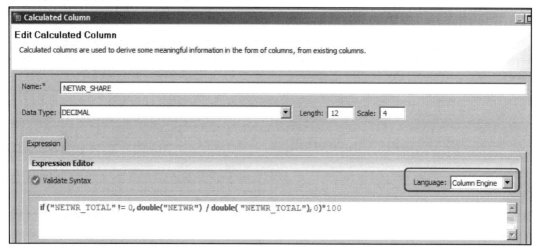

Note: Click on "Validate Syntax" to verify the correctness of formula before closing this window

3.3.3 Key points about calculated columns:

- **Conditional expression using IF vs CASE**
  Use CASE expression instead of IF, when there are multiple levels of conditions. Nested IF conditions are difficult to interpret and sometimes they may produce inaccurate results.

  CASE – SQL engine

  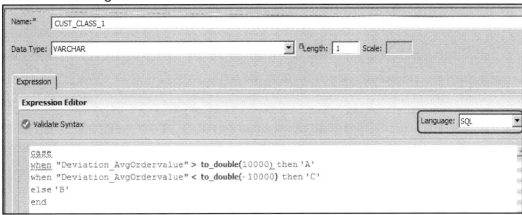

  IF – Column engine

  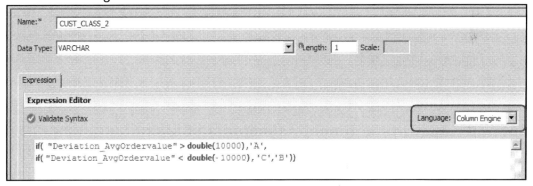

  Results: Observe the results for both the formulas. They are matching here.

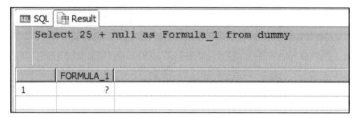

- **Null value treatment between SQL and Column engine**
  Null values are used to represent Un-defined values of a field. HANA also supports the Null values like other databases. We need to consider few aspects while performing calculations or operations on the Null values.

  In SQL engine-based formulas always ensure that the operands are not NULL values, while implementing arithmetic operations. Because the result will be also NULL if there is any operand as NULL. However, when we implement this formula using Calculation engine, the NULL value will be interpreted as 0.

  ```
  Select 25 + null as Formula_1 from dummy
  ```

	FORMULA_1
1	?

  How to fix the above issue We can use the ifnull() function to verify if the operator is NULL and set its value accordingly.

  ```
  Select 25 + ifnull(null,0) as Formula_1 from dummy
  ```

	FORMULA_1
1	25

- **Data Type conversion scenarios**
  Always ensure to implement necessary data type conversions during the formula processing, to ensure that the formula will give accurate results. We can achieve this by using the SQL engine functions such as to_int(), to_date(), or the Column engine function such as int(), date()

52

3.3.4 Implementing Count Type Measures

In various KPI requirements, we are supposed to count the number of values in an attribute, such as the number of purchase orders which are delivered late. The other common requirement is to count the distinct values of an attribute, such as distinct number of customers for the sales orders in a given period.

We can use the following methods to address the requirements related to count type measures

1) Setting the aggregation property of an attribute to "Count" in an aggregation node

   Example: Count of distinct customers in sales orders

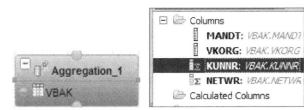 

2) Calculating the occurrences using a formula (using a calculated column)

   Example: Count_Of_Open_Orders

   Formula: if (Order_Status = 'Open', 1, 0)

3) We can use Counter type of calculated columns (measures) to derive distinct count for a combination of attributes. Counters can be only implemented in the final aggregation / projection node of a calculation view.

Example: Define a "Counter" type calculated measure for "Count Distinct" of Customers

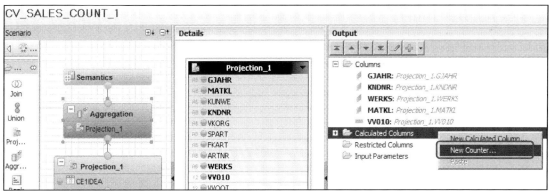

Create the following counter under calculated columns (Count of Distinct KNDNR)

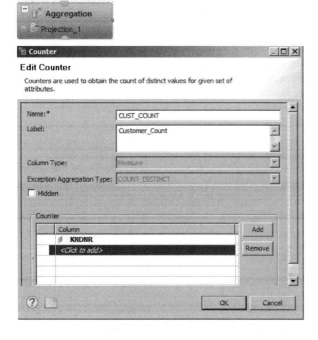

Verify the results of the Count Distinct measure

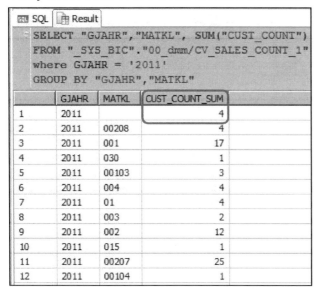

When we perform the Count Distinct at a different aggregation level (Fiscal year level) for specific selection of Material Groups, we can see that the distinct set of customers are calculated accordingly

```
SELECT "GJAHR", SUM("CUST_COUNT") AS "CUST_COUNT_SUM"
FROM "_SYS_BIC"."00_dmm/CV_SALES_COUNT_1"
where GJAHR = '2011' and MATKL in ('00207','00208')
GROUP BY "GJAHR"
```

	GJAHR	CUST_COUNT_SUM
1	2011	26

Behavior of Counter Measures in Stacked views – Using the Transparent Filter Option:

When we try to query the counter measures which are defined in the inner calculation views of a stacked model, the results may not be accurate due to the aggregation behavior.

For example, the below query on the main calculation view is producing different (incorrect) result when we compare with the query on the inner calculation view where the counter measure is defined.

In the below query we can observe that the Distinct count is incorrect.

```
SELECT "GJAHR", SUM("CUST_COUNT") AS "CUST_COUNT_SUM"
FROM "_SYS_BIC"."00_dmm/CV_SALES_COUNT_MAIN"
where GJAHR = '2011' and MATKL in ('00207','00208')
GROUP BY "GJAHR"
```

	GJAHR	CUST_COUNT_SUM
1	2011	29

To overcome this issue, we shall use the "Transparent Filter" property on the respective attributes (Material Group in this case).

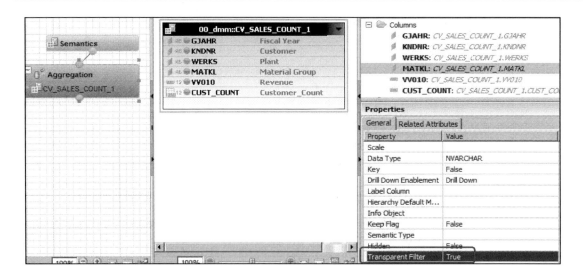

We need to apply the Transparent Filter property in the inner calculation view (where the Counter Measure is defined) also

Results after the "Transparent Filter" setting: It is producing correct results now.

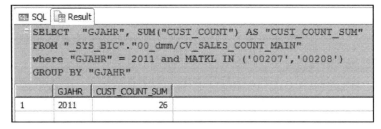

Limitations of Counter Measures:

- Counter measures can only be defined at the final Aggregation node. Also, we cannot use the Counter Measure inside the definition of a calculated column of the same aggregation node.

  To address the challenges related to the above limitations, we need to implement stacked calculation views. In this approach, implement the Counter measures in the inner calculation view and use them subsequently in the main calculation view

- We cannot apply any filters specifically on Counter Measures. For example, you need to perform the Count of Purchase Orders which are having the status as "Open". To address this, we need to create the calculated columns as explained already.

3.3.5 Time Dimension

Time Dimensions will play an important role in modeling HANA views, since most of the transactional data is generally associated with specific dates and time periods. While running the reports, it is very common to filter the results for specific period such as Calendar Month, Fiscal Year, Fiscal Week etc. Hence the time dimension attributes are an essential means of filtering the transaction data which is processed in the view.

While creating calculation views in HANA we can choose the sub type as "Time" to implement a time dimension view.

Steps:

Create calculation view of type Time

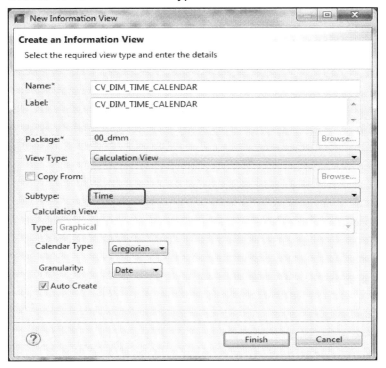

Calendar Type:

Gregorian:
- Provides regular Calendar year attributes (Calendar Month, Calendar Quarter etc.)
- It will be always January to December

Fiscal:
- Financial calendar specific to the organization (Fiscal Period, Fiscal Week etc.)
- Always linked with an attribute call Fiscal year variant, which will have the setup of the fiscal year

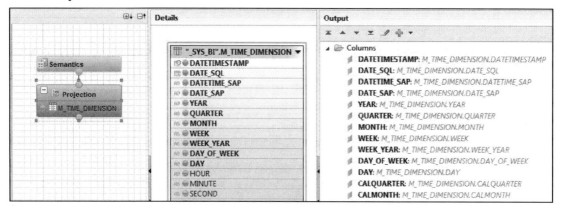

Generate Time Data:

This is a one-time activity which can be performed in the Quick View tools of the HANA modeling perspective. After the Generate Time Data is run, the data is populated into the standard tables which is accessed via the views like M_TIME_DIEMSION (Gregorian), M_TIME_FISCAL (Fiscal)

Data Preview:

DATE_SQL	DATETIME_SAP	DATE_SAP	YEAR	QUARTER	MONTH	WEEK
Oct 1, 2018	20181001000000	20181001	2018	04	10	40
Oct 8, 2018	20181008000000	20181008	2018	04	10	41
Oct 15, 2018	20181015000000	20181015	2018	04	10	42
Oct 22, 2018	20181022000000	20181022	2018	04	10	43
Oct 29, 2018	20181029000000	20181029	2018	04	10	44
Nov 5, 2018	20181105000000	20181105	2018	04	11	45
Nov 12, 2018	20181112000000	20181112	2018	04	11	46
Nov 19, 2018	20181119000000	20181119	2018	04	11	47
Nov 26, 2018	20181126000000	20181126	2018	04	11	48
Dec 1, 2018	20181201000000	20181201	2018	04	12	48
Dec 3, 2018	20181203000000	20181203	2018	04	12	49

Joining the Time Dimension

Please note that all the date fields from SAP application tables or BW data targets are generated in HANA as NVARCHAR(8) type fields. Hence, we need to follow the below approach while joining with the Time Dimensions in Calculation views.

Field in Time Dimension	Data Type	Format	Usage
DATE_SQL	DATE	YYYY-MM-DD	To use as a proper DATE column in HANA models
DATE_SAP	NVARCHAR	YYYYMMDD	To join the Date Fields from SAP tables which are represented as NVARCHAR(8)
CALENDAR_VARIANT	NVARCHAR	Example 'K4'	To filter the Fiscal based time dimension on specific Fiscal Year Variant

Persisting the Time Dimension Values

It would be greatly beneficial to have the persisted attributes of Date Dimension with additional fields that can help in addressing common data modeling requirements such as "Rolling <N> months", "Year to Date", "Previous Year" etc. We can achieve this by implementing a custom table in HANA which is updated periodically (typically once in a day) by using a SQL script stored procedure.

Below is an example of such custom table, where we are adding the new fields with the relative calculations, we can achieve this. We can use this table while defining various KPIs which are based on time dimension.

DATE_SQL	CALMONTH	CALYEAR	RELATIVE_CALMONTH	RELATIVE_YEAR	RELATIVE_FISCPER
15-03-2018	201803	2018	0	0	0
15-02-2018	201802	2018	-1	0	0
10-05-2018	201805	2018	2	0	0
10-03-2017	201703	2017	-12	-1	-1

KPI Examples:

1) Rolling 3 Months Sales Revenue.
   Filter criteria: RELATIVE_CALMONTH between -3 and -1
2) Year To Date.
   Filter criteria: RELATIVE_CALYEAR = 0 and RELATIVE_DATE <=0

Data flow for implementing derived date dimensions in SAP HANA:

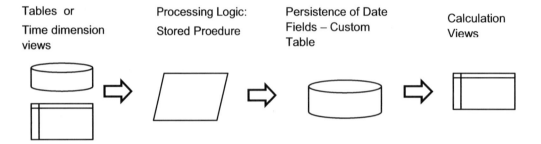

3.4 Calculation View Semantics

We can maintain various semantic properties for the calculation view both at the view level and at the individual column level. Sematic properties are mainly used to control the display or processing behavior of the columns (For example: Field label, No of decimal places). Let us go through some of the important semantic properties and their importance

3.4.1 Currency and Unit Conversions

Currency Conversions

As a pre-requisite the following tables need to be in the replication to perform Currency Conversions in HANA models.
TCURC, TCURX, TCURF, TCURR, TCURT, TCURV

Generally, these conversion tables are replicated from ECC or S/4 HANA and addressed from the respective schema. We can apply currency conversion on the measures using the following settings. Ensure that the Default Schema is set to the Schema which has the Currency Conversion tables.

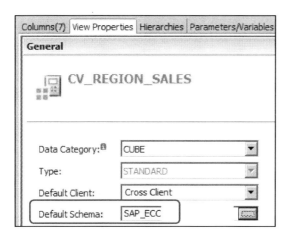

Requirement: We need to convert all the values of Sales Order Net value into commonly reporting currency such as USD.

In this example, we are creating a calculated column based on Net value (NETWR) and applying currency conversion to derive all the values in USD.

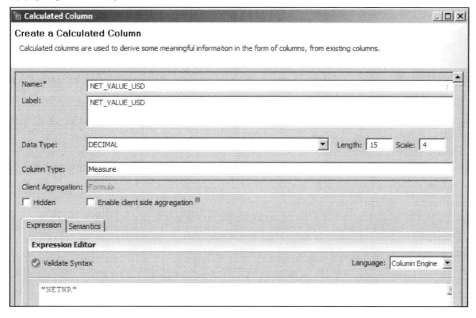

Switch to the Semantics tab and choose the type as "Amount with currency".

Enter the Currency Conversion settings for this column.

In this example we are converting all the values to USD.

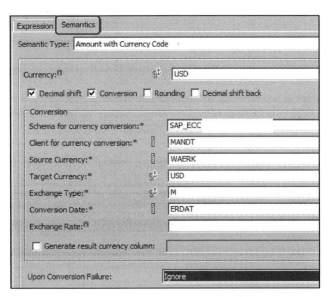

Note: We can choose the parameters like Source / Target Currency, Client, Exchange rate from the table columns, or as fixed values are from Input Parameters

Unit Conversions:

As a pre-requisite the following tables need to be in the replication to perform Unit Conversions in HANA models: T006, T006A

We shall use the following methods to perform Unit Conversion in HANA:

- To perform unit conversions between the unit of measures which are of same dimension (Example: Kilo Gram to Tonne, Litres to Gallons):
    - Use the standard unit conversion feature in the calculation view semantic properties.
    - We need to specify the Source unit / Target unit
- To perform unit conversions between the unit of measures which belongs to different dimension (Example Cases to Palettes, Each to Cases etc): Use the SAP standard table MARM which provides the numerator and denominator to perform the conversion into alternate unit of measures.

3.4.2 Hierarchies

Hierarchies allow the users to perform drill down the KPIs during the report in a flexible manner. HANA supports the following two types of hierarchies, which can be created in the Dimension type calculation views.

Level Hierarchy: To represent the relationship between different attributes of a Dimension in hierarchical format. Generally, we will implement level hierarchies when the attributes are of heterogenous type.

Example: Level Hierarchy on Calendar Dimension attributes

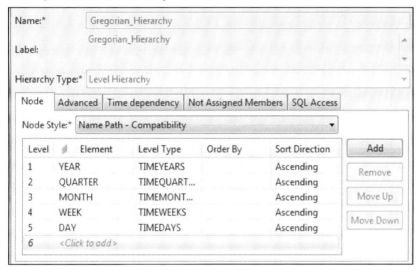

Parent Child Hierarchy: To represent the relationship between different attributes of a Dimension in hierarchical format. Generally, we will implement parent child hierarchies when the attributes are of same type

Examples: Employee and Manager
            Assembly product and Component Product

3.4.3 Star Join Calculation Views

Star Join type calculation views are the replacement to analytic views. In this we will join a set of transactional tables from the data foundation to a group of dimension views that connects the master data attributes. At runtime the start join is executed by the OLAP engine, which provides optimal processing for summarizing results.

Additional features of Star Join type views
- Supports Temporal Joins: This will allow the reporting of time-dependent master data in a calculation view
- SQL Access of Hierarchies – We can run the queries based on Hierarchy Node also

Few limitations with Star join calculation views:
- We can only use the Dimension Type calculation views as the dimensions in the start join node. We cannot directly join database tables and other possible data sources.
- We cannot reuse the same dimension view more than once in the star join. For example, if we need to have two separate dimensions for Customer (Sold_To and Ship_To), we need to create two different Dimension type calculation views and use them.

3.4.4 Stacked Calculation Views

Calculation views are the common type of views on which the final reporting solutions are implemented in the HANA data mart projects. While designing the solution for individual KPI requirements, we need to consider the modular approach for the creation of calculation views which is also known as stacked calculation views.

Advantages of implementing stacked calculation views:

- ✓ Creation of smaller reusable calculation views

- ✓ Ease of maintenance and troubleshooting – we can make the changes to only specific calculation views in a stacked model and the data validations will be easier to perform.

- ✓ To achieve complex business calculations, such as the count and percentage operations which need to be performed at different levels of a model

- ✓ Flexibility to implement appropriate type of calculation views such as Dimension type for master data and Cube type for the aggregations or to generate the final output as per the requirements

3.4.5 Value Help Views

Value help view are basically calculation views, built to provide input help (Similar to F4 help in SAP environment) in the form of list of values that can be chosen for a specific attribute, during the user prompt for any variable or input parameter.

When the end user runs a report and trying to enter input values (for variables or input parameters), by default the popup will try to provide the values from the same calculation view. Since this may cause long run time to fetch the distinct values from the transaction data, it is ideal to implement separate calculation views as value help views. These value help views can be reused across multiple calculation views for the variables or input parameter prompts which are based on the similar attribute.

Procedure:

- Create a calculation view CV_LOV_PLANT for Plant values based on table T001W
- Assign CV_LOV_PLANT as the Value help view in the definition of input parameters or variables

3.4.6 Controlling Aggregation Behavior using KEEP flag

Whenever a query is run on a calculation view, all the measures are aggregated for the combination of attributes which are requested in the query. After that the calculated columns are derived by executing the formulas. This is the ideal processing behavior to achieve optimal performance as well.

However, in specific cases, the result of formula will not be appropriate when it is performed after the aggregation. For example, calculating the Revenue = Quantity * Price. This formula must be run at the respective document line item level to ensure that the calculation is performed before aggregating the respective measures involved in the formula (Quantity and Price in this case). We can achieve this by setting the Keep Flag = True for those attributes which are supposed to be part of the query to perform the calculations.

In nutshell, the Keep Flag property is used to ensure that certain attributes should be always included in the query on a view even when those attributes are not requested in the query. Enabling the Keep Flag property on the attributes will lead to slow performance, since it will lead to the processing of larger data set.

3.4.7 Flexibility in join operations using Dynamic Joins

Normally when we implement a join between two nodes, we will specify the set of columns which are involved in the join condition. While processing the join node the join condition is executed by comparing all these fields even if we have not requested them in the query.

However, in specific cases, we would like to have the flexibility in join execution during runtime, which means the join condition should be applied on only those columns which are requested in the query. This will allow us to build flexible modeling solutions. We can achieve this functionality in HANA by setting the Dynamic Join property, which is available in Inner Join only.

Example: Business Case: Sales Revenue Percentage Share Calculations

3.5 Best Practices for implementing Calculation Views

3.5.1 Performance Optimization Techniques

Filters: Effective means of reducing the data sets to be processed

- ✓ Reduce the data set as early as possible. Use design time filters at the lowest level possible

- ✓ Ensure that the variables (where clause) are pushed to the lowest level on the respective tables. Verify this using Plan Visualizer

- ✓ Strictly avoid filters or join conditions based on calculated columns. Filters applied on the calculated columns will not be pushed down to the database, which can lead to huge data volumes to be processed during the query runtime.

  For example, we need to apply the filter on the "Fiscal Year", which is the first 4 characters of the "Posting Date" column. Following are the recommended options to address this.

  - Identify any other data source from which we can derive this column (Fiscal Year) by joining with the table which has the column with the actual values (Posting Date) and implement the necessary joins to derive the column

  - Try to persist these columns in the table level either during the ETL process or within HANA

- ✓ Use analytical privileges to filter data whenever possible since they act as filters on the source table.

Joins:

- ✓ Use left outer joins as much as possible to take the advantage of "Join Pruning".

- ✓ Implement the Text Joins at the top layer, where the records are minimal

- ✓ Specify cardinality in joins (n:1 or 1:1) – only when it is known

- ✓ Set optimize join = true (when cardinality is set as mentioned above)

- ✓ Try to avoid join conditions based on calculated columns (better options to persist these calculated columns in the table level).

- ✓ Processing of joins on columns with either INTEGER or BIGINT data types will be efficient over the columns of Character types

Aggregation / Calculations:

- ✓ Aggregations are generally time consuming when the number of attributes and measures increases.

- ✓ Avoid aggregation on very large set of records, since it can be very time consuming and consumes lot of memory - Consider the following options:

  - ○ Try to filter the records before aggregation

  - ○ Split the records into multiple aggregation nodes with smaller set of records

- ✓ Always try to implement the Calculated Columns at the aggregation level

- ✓ Handle the NULL values properly within the formulas

General Recommendations:

- ✓ Avoid transferring large result sets between HANA DB and client applications (e.g. Lumira or Web Intelligence etc.)
- ✓ Avoid implementing calculations in the front-end reporting tools, always prefer to implement them in the HANA view itself
- ✓ Use table functions instead of scripted calculation views.

- ✓ Try to leverage "Execute in SQL-engine" option for Stacked calculation views. Sometimes this will lead to improvement in performance

3.5.2 Best practice to perform changes to HANA modeling artifacts

While implementing any changes to the HANA information views, consider below options to ensure the consistency and ease of maintaining the views.

- For simpler changes: Maintain back up copy of the respective views before implementing the changes in the original views

    Examples:

    Adding new attributes, measures and formulas to the existing nodes

    Changing the formulas, semantics such as currency conversions, hierarchies etc.

- For complex changes: Make a copy of the main views in a test package, implement the changes to the copies and validate results before moving the changes to the main package

    Examples:

    Adding new nodes between the existing nodes

    Re-designing the existing data flow

- Leverage the development perspective options such as Check out, Reset to Active and Remove from Client

3.6 Calculation View Examples

Let us go through some of the sample business cases and KPI requirements and learn the various approaches to build solutions using the calculation views.

3.6.1 Business Case: Sales order analysis and customer classification

Requirement description: Classification of customers based on total order value for the past periods as per the selection.

1) Create a Graphical calculation view (type – Cube) based on KNA1 and VBAK tables

2) Apply static filters: Sales Document type VBAK-VBTYP = 'C' (Sales orders)

3) Implement the join between KNA1 and VBAK – Join condition is based on KUNNR and MANDT

4) Create a Calculated column "Customer_Class" based on the below logic:

   a. If the total revenue (VBAK-NETWR) between 0 to 10000 – 'Silver'
   b. If the total revenue (VBAK-NETWR) between 10000 to 50000 – 'Gold'
   c. If the total revenue (VBAK-NETWR) more than 50000 – 'Platinum'

5) Create a counter measure for Number of sales orders (Distinct Count on VBAK-VBELN)

6) User input – Define following variables:

   a. Var_Sales_Org (Label: Sales Organization)(Filter on: VBAK-VKORG)
      Type = Single Value and Optional
   b. Var_Doc_Date (Label: Sales doc date) (Filter on: VBAK-ERDAT)
      Type = Range and Mandatory

7) Create a calculation view (type Dimension) for Value help on Sales org (use the master data tables of sales org – TVKO) and assign to the variable

Sample Layout:

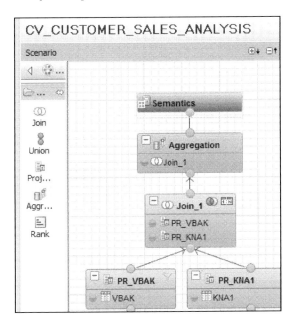

Detailed Solution Steps:

1. Create a new calculation view with the following properties.
   In the HANA development perspective, switch to the Repository tab. Right click on the package and choose the following option to create a new calculation view.

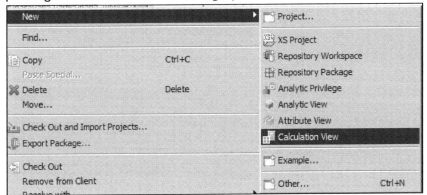

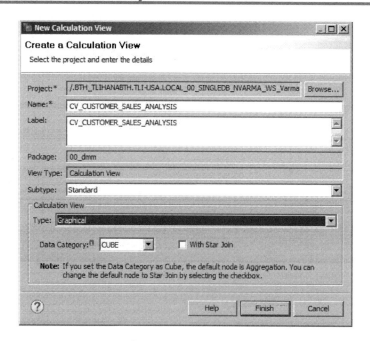

2. Add two projections and rename Projection_1 as PR_VBAK and Projection_2 as PR_KNA1

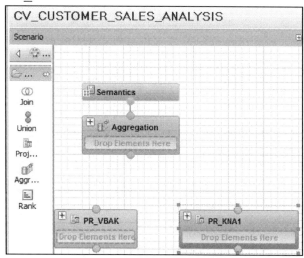

3. On Projections click on '+' symbol and add the table VBAK in Projection_Sale and KNA1table in Projection_Cust as well.
Note: Both these tables are to be added from appropriate Schema.

SAP® HANA Modeling Practical World — Calculation Views - Modeling Techniques

Add the following fields to the output of both the projection nodes

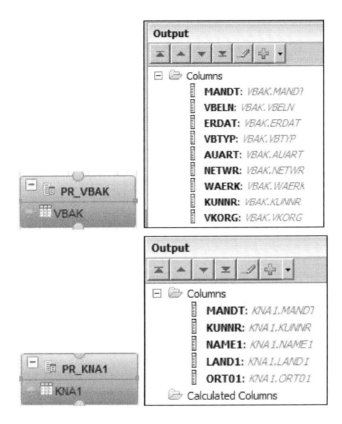

Apply the filter on VBTYP field of Projection PR_VBAK (To fetch only Sales Orders)

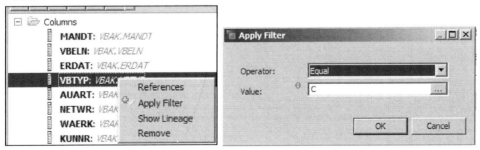

4. Add a Join node in the model
   Select the fields from VBAK and KNA1 tables and implement join as shown below
   (Join type: Left outer join)

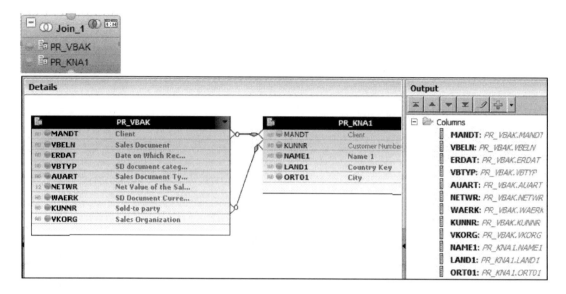

5. Connect the Join_1 node to the final Aggregation and add the fields (attributes and measures) to the output.
   Note: We need to add NETWR using – Add as aggregated column, since it is a measure

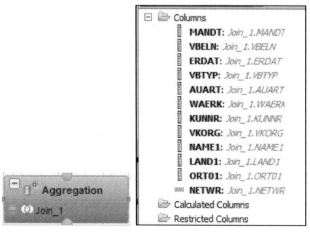

SAP® HANA Modeling Practical World — Calculation Views - Modeling Techniques

Add a calculated column CUSTOMER_CLASS as shown below

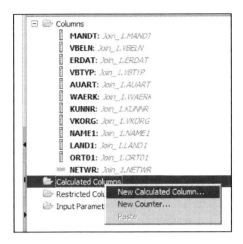

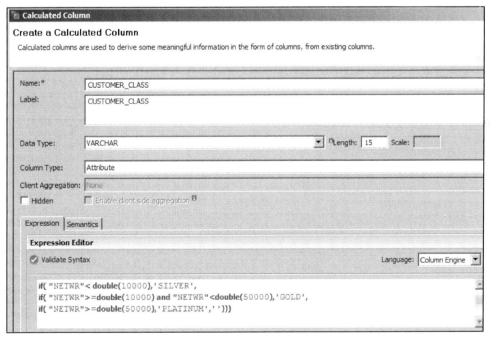

SAP® HANA Modeling Practical World — Calculation Views - Modeling Techniques

6. Maintain column level semantics as shown below
   Label, setting the type as Attribute or Measure

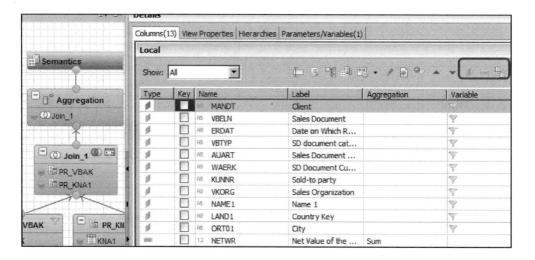

7. Create the variables for Input selection with ranges for Creation date (ERDAT) and Sale Organization (VKORG) as shown below.

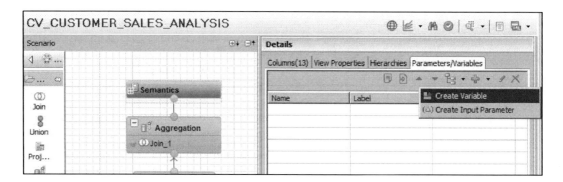

| SAP® HANA Modeling Practical World | Calculation Views - Modeling Techniques |

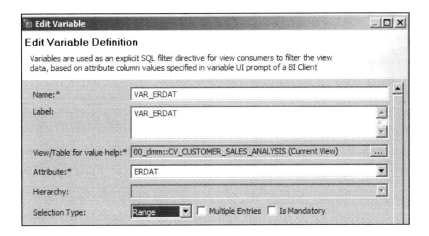

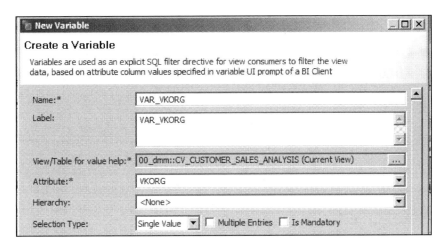

Save and activate the view.

8. Create a Value Help View: To Provide Input values for Sale Organization:
   Create a calculation view (CV_LOV_SALES_ORG) data category as DIMENSION
   Source table: TVKO (Sales organizations)
   View Type: DIMENSION

SAP® HANA Modeling Practical World — Calculation Views - Modeling Techniques

Implement the value help view as shown below.

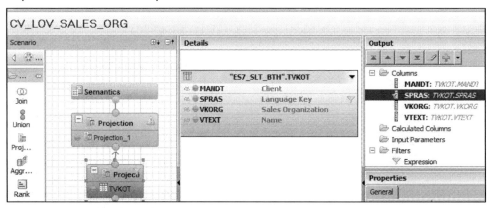

Set filter on SPRAS (Language) = E

Now change the variable field(VAR_VKORG) in Bfor sales organization and provide the calculation and provide the calculation view name(CV_LOV_SALES_ORG) as Value help for this variable.

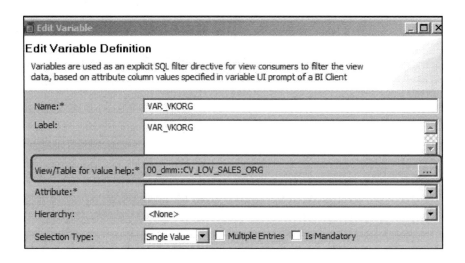

Choose the value help view as shown above.
Save and activate the view.

Validate the results of Calculation view:

Run data preview to see the results of the calculation view.
Enter appropriate values for the variables.
VAR_ERDAT – 20130101 to 20131231
VAR_VKORG – 3020

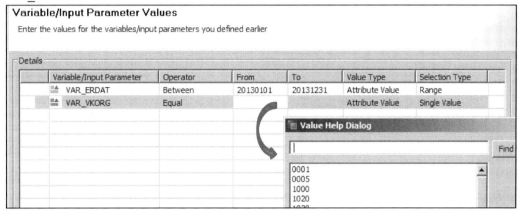

Note: Variable help dialog for VAR_VKORG is generated from the Value Help view CV_LOV_SALES_ORG as shown above.

Validate the results and check if the CUSTOMER_CLASS is derived correctly.

VKORG	KUNNR	NAME1	LAND1	CUSTOMER_CLASS	NETWR_SUM
3020	0000000481	Peter King	US	PLATINUM	20,563,690.15
3020	0000000481	Peter King	US	SILVER	0
3020	0000003271	Media Store	US	GOLD	20,033
3020	0000003271	Media Store	US	SILVER	3,603.1
3020	0000003272	ADCOM CO...	US	PLATINUM	200,330
3020	0000003273	ALPHA Center	US	SILVER	0
3020	0000003279	Tech Store	US	PLATINUM	748,617.5
3020	0000003360	Anderson M...	US	GOLD	79,535
3020	0000003360	Anderson M...	US	PLATINUM	90,820

| SAP® HANA Modeling | Calculation Views - Modeling Techniques |
| Practical World | |

3.6.2 Business Case: Derive Material Status based on Plant level status

Requirement: To get the distinct set materials along with the "Material Status" based on the following criteria:

- When the material has status as 'DC' for all the plants, set the "Material_Status" to 'Discontinued'
- When the material has status as 'AC' in any of the plants, set the "Material_Status" to 'Active', otherwise when the material has status as 'RD' in any of the plants, set the "Material_Status" to 'Rampdown'

Source Table:

Select * from nvarma.mat_plant

	MATERIAL	PLANT	PLAN_DAYS	STATUS
1	MAT1	1000	12	AC
2	MAT1	2000	15	RD
3	MAT2	1000	10	RD
4	MAT2	2000	7	DC
5	MAT2	3000	5	RD
6	MAT3	1000	30	DC
7	MAT3	2000	20	DC

Expected Result:

MATERIAL	MATERIAL_STATUS
MAT1	Active
MAT2	RampDown
MAT3	Discontinued

Solution Details:

1   Create a DIMENSION Type calculation view
    View name: CV_DIM_MAT_STATUS
    Data Category: DIMENSION

2   Build the nodes in the calculation view as per the layout given below

2.1   Projection node on MAT_PLANT table

| SAP® HANA Modeling Practical World | Calculation Views - Modeling Techniques |

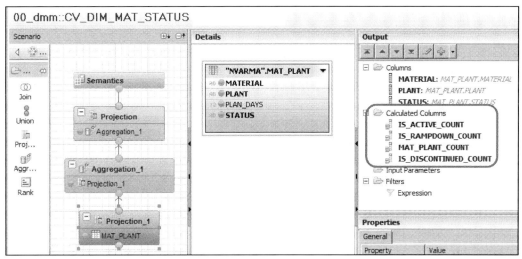

Add the fields to output – Material, Plant and Status

Create the following Calculated columns:

IS_ACTIVE_COUNT (INTEGER): Formula: if ("STATUS" = 'AC', 1, 0)

IS_RAMPDOWN_COUNT (INTEGER): Formula: if ("STATUS" = 'RD', 1, 0)

IS_RAMPDOWN_COUNT (INTEGER): Formula: if ("STATUS" = 'RD', 1, 0)

IS_DISCONTINUED_COUNT (INTEGER): Formula: if ("STATUS" = 'DC', 1, 0)

MAT_PLANT_COUNT (INTEGER): Formula: 1

2.2 Aggregation node to derive the Material status

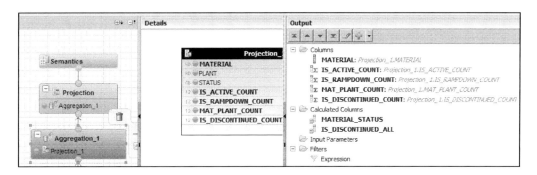

81

Implementing Calculated columns

MATERIAL_STATUS (VARCHAR 20):

```
case
when "IS_ACTIVE_COUNT" > 0 then 'Active'
when "IS_RAMPDOWN_COUNT" > 0 then 'RampDown'
when "IS_DISCONTINUED_COUNT" = "MAT_PLANT_COUNT" then 'Discontinued'
else 'NA'
end
```

Note: In the above CASE statement, it will not support the expression to compare one field with another (`when "IS_DISCONTINUED_COUNT" = "MAT_PLANT_COUNT"`).

Workaround: Create a new calculated column in the same node
IS_DISCONTINUED_ALL
Formula: if (`"MAT_PLANT_COUNT" = "IS_DISCONTINUED_COUNT"`, 1, 0)

Revise the CASE statement as below.

```
case
when "IS_ACTIVE_COUNT" > 0 then 'Active'
when "IS_RAMPDOWN_COUNT" > 0 then 'RampDown'
when "IS_DISCONTINUED_ALL" > 0 then 'Discontinued'
else 'NA'
end
```

2.3   Semantics – final output columns

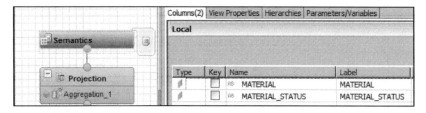

2.4   Output of the calculation view – We can observe that the MATERIAL_STATUS is derived as per the requirement

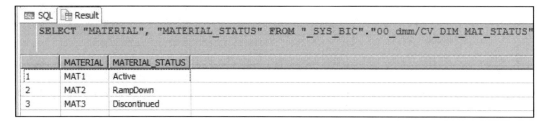

82

3.6.3 Business Case: Implement Sales Employee Hierarchy Dimension View

Requirement: Create Dimension view for Employee details along with the Supervisor number and name. Implement Parent Child hierarchy to show the relationship of each employee and the supervisor. This view can be reused in various reporting views to show the employee hierarchy details.

Key Learnings:

- Dimension Type Calculation View
- Parent Child hierarchies

Calculation view layout for Employee Master data:

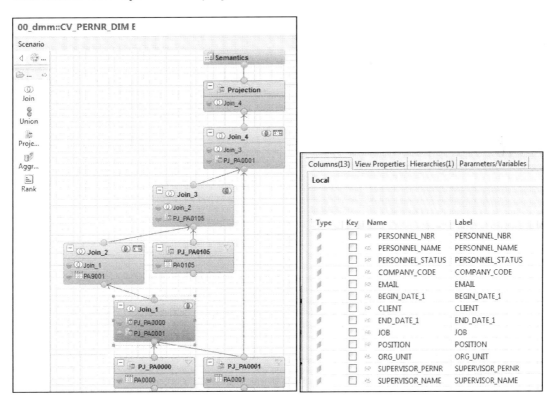

Source Tables:

- PA0000 - Employee master record
- PA0001 - Employee name, address
- PA0005 - Employee Number and corresponding SAP User ID
- PA9001 – Employee and Supervisor relationship

Set the Data Category to **Dimension** in the View Properties.

Projection on PA0000 table:

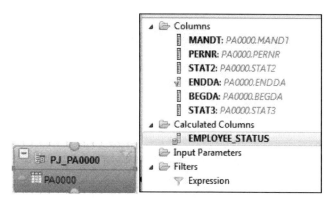
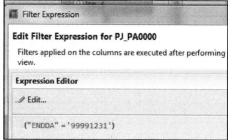

Calculated column for Employee Status:

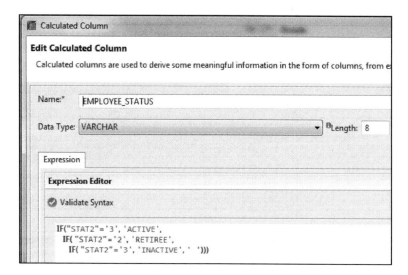

Projection on PA0001 table: To derive Employee details along with the name

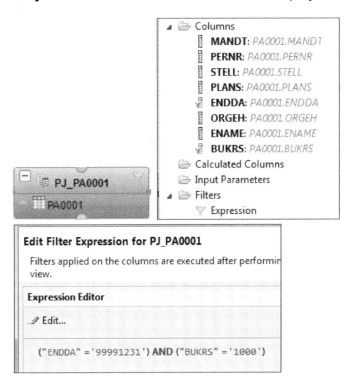

Join on PA0000 and PA0001: To derive employee name (Inner join)

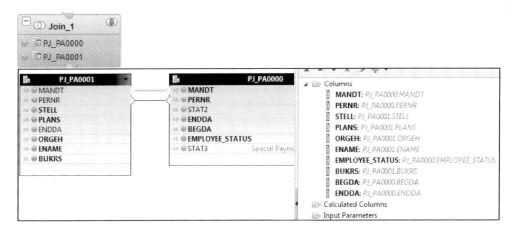

Join with PA9001 table: To derive Supervisor Number – SPERNR (Inner Join)

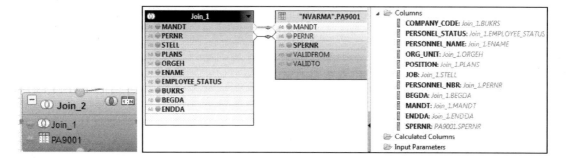

Projection on PA0105 table: To derive SAP User ID for the employee numbers

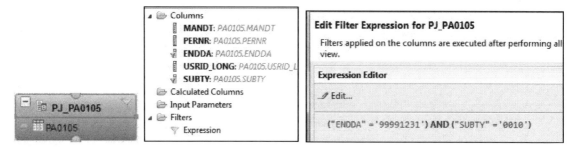

Join with PA0105 table: To derive SAP User ID (Left Outer Join)

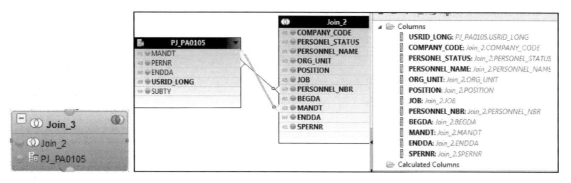

Join with PA0001 table: To derive Supervisor Employee Name (Left Outer Join)

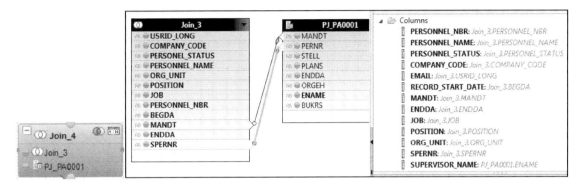

Final Projection node:

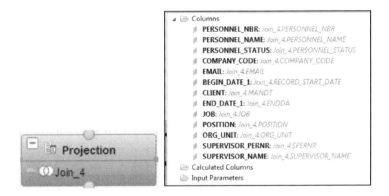

Implement the following Parent / Child hierarchy:

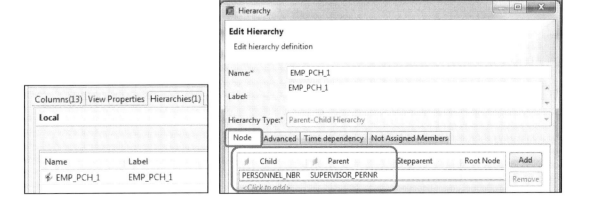

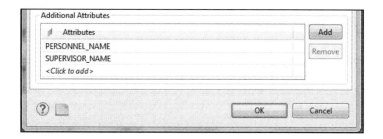

Maintain Time Dependency settings:

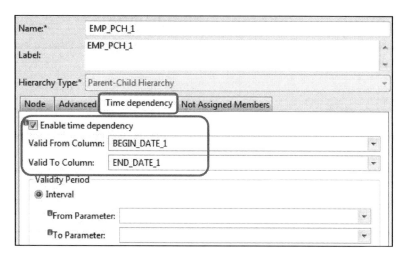

Data preview:

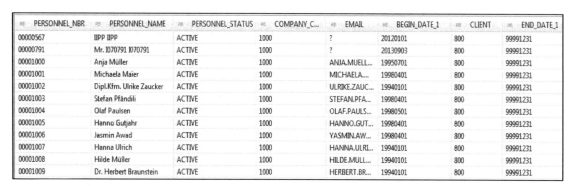

3.6.4 Business Case: Display Revenue by Sales Employee Hierarchy

Requirement: Implement a calculation view to show the Sales revenue based on employee hierarchy. This view should allow the reporting users to drill down the sales revenue accomplished by the employees at different levels of the organizational hierarchy

Key Learnings:

- Star Join Calculation View
- Parent Child hierarchies
- Implementing temporal joins to address time-dependent master data reporting
- Querying results based on Hierarchy nodes using SQL access option

Layout of Calculation view:

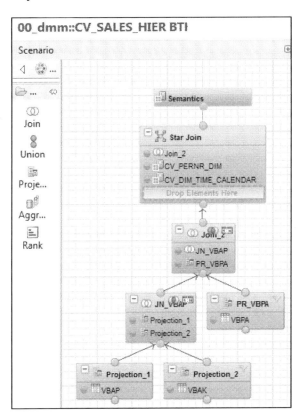

Implement the following join on VBAP and VBAK table: (Inner Join)

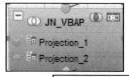

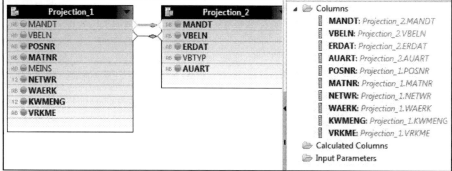

Projection node on VBPA: Apply the following filter to bring only Sales Persons

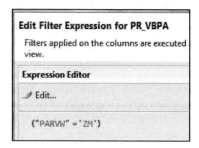

Join_2: Join with VBPA table to Business Partners (Sales Employee) – (Left Outer Join)

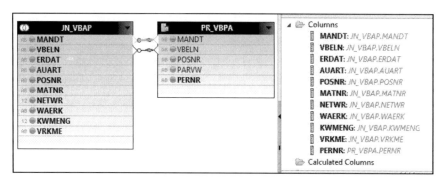

SAP® HANA Modeling Practical World — Calculation Views - Modeling Techniques

Star Join Node:

Add the following dimension views: CV_PERNR_DIM and CV_DIM_TIME_DIMENSION

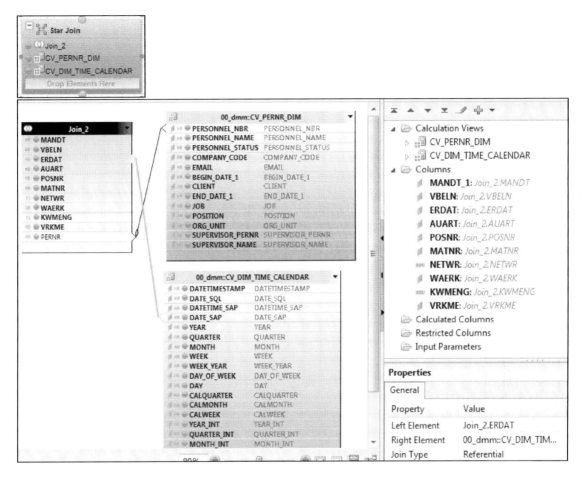

Implement temporal join on Employee dimension:

SAP® HANA Modeling Practical World — Calculation Views - Modeling Techniques

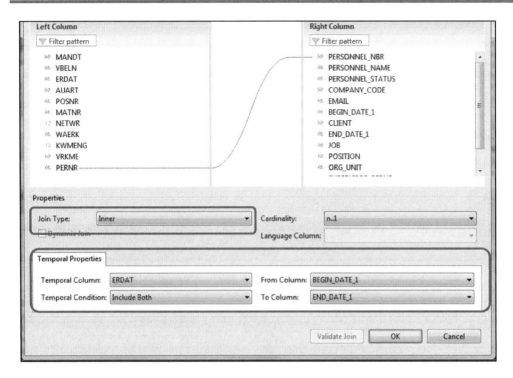

Ensure to set the property "Enable Hierarchies for SQL access" in the view properties

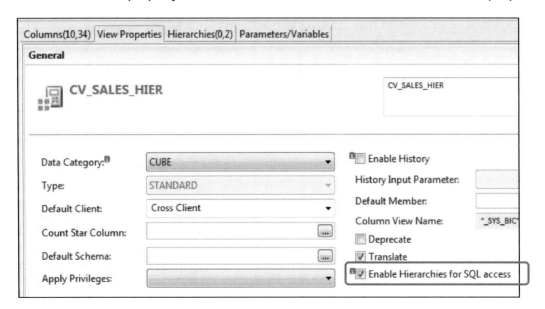

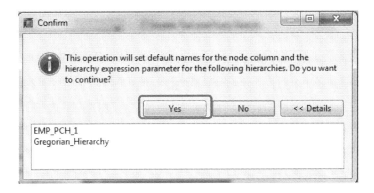

Confirm the above popup with **Yes**

Go to the Hierarchies tab and set the properties including the SQL access related.

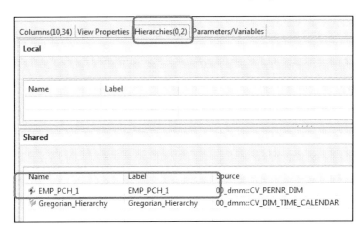

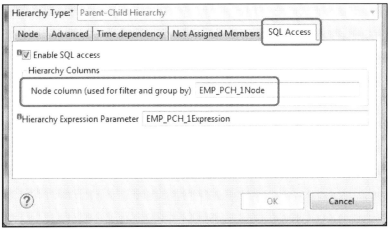

Advantage of SQL Access – generated Hierarchy Node column:

- We can use this column in the GROUP BY or WHERE Clause of a Select query on this calculation view.
- We can also use this column in the definition of Analytic privileges to allow the row level access to the data based on hierarchy nodes.

Note: We can use the virtual table called BIMC_HIERARCHIES to verify the definition of hierarchies.

MDX select HIERARCHY_NAME, NODE_COLUMN_NAME, CUBE_NAME from BIMC_HIERARCHIES where HIERARCHY_NAME = 'EMP_PCH_1'

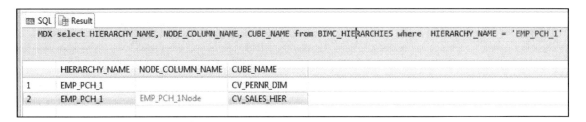

BIMC_HIERARCHIES table is a virtual table. It does not exist physically. The metadata containing the results from a "SELECT from BIMC_HIERARCHIES" statement is held inside internal data structures and a result set for the SELECT statement is constructed from those internal data structures and not from an SQL table.

SAP® HANA Modeling Practical World | Calculation Views - Modeling Techniques

3.6.5 Business Case: Sales Revenue YTD and MTD calculations

Requirement: An organization wants to view the sales revenue for various time periods such as Month to Date (MTD) and Year To Date (YTD) and Rolling 3 months – based on the CO PA sales perofrmance actuals (CE1IDEA Table)

Key features of the solution include:
- ✓ Implementing Input Parameters – (Derived from table)
- ✓ Projection Filter expressions
- ✓ Union node to merge the source records with different set of measures

Graphical View and Sample result:

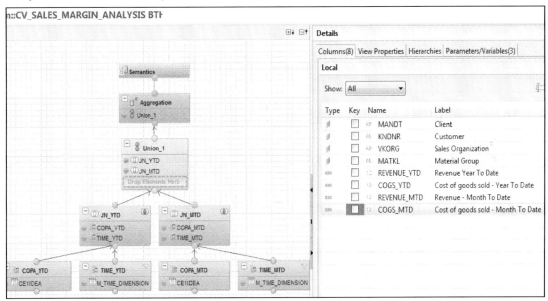

Below are the detailed definition of nodes to be implemented in this calculation view:

Projection COPA_YTD: Derive required fields from CE1IDEA

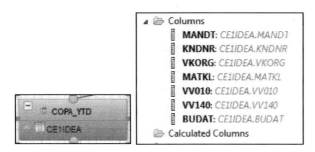

Projection COPA_MTD: Derive required fields from CE1IDEA

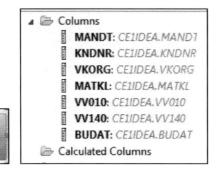

Projection TIME_YTD: Implement filter to apply restrictions as per Year To Date logic

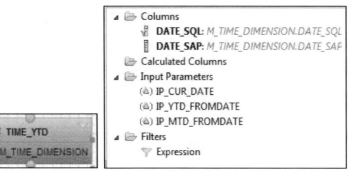

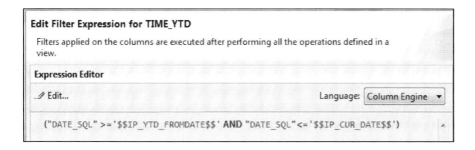

Projection TIME_MTD: Implement filter to apply restrictions as per Month To Date logic

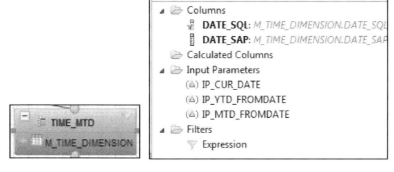

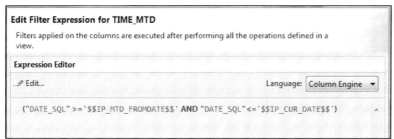

To derive the values of certain date dimension related fields such as the YTD From Date, we have to create a table similar to this and populate it using a stored procedure.

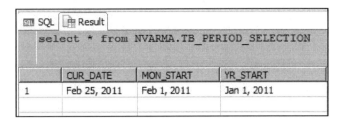

Create the following input parameters:

1) Input Parameter Name: IP_CUR_DATE

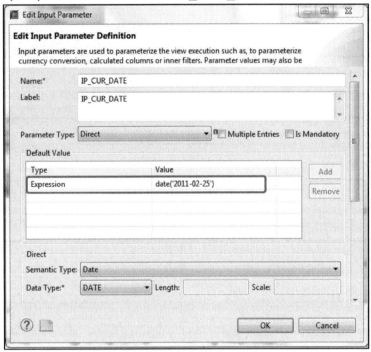

2) Input Parameter Name: IP_MTDFROMDATE
   Parameter Type : Derived from table

| SAP® HANA Modeling Practical World | Calculation Views - Modeling Techniques |

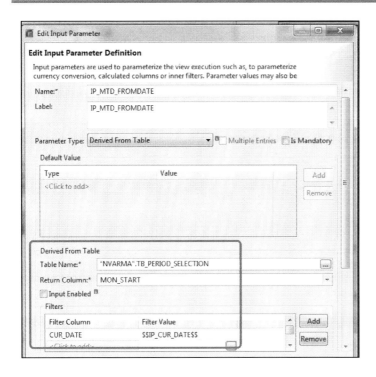

3) Input Parameter Name: IP_YTDFROMDATE (Similar to the above)
   Parameter Type : Derived from table
   Table: TB_PERIOD_SELECTIN (From the appropriate Schema)
   Return Column: YR_START
   Filter Column: CUR_DATE
   Filter Value: $$IP_CUR_DATE$$

Join the COPA_YTD projection with TIME_YTD projection: (Inner join)

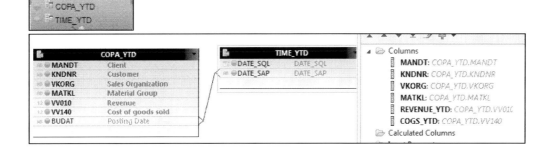

99

SAP® HANA Modeling Practical World — Calculation Views - Modeling Techniques

Join the COPA_MTD projection with TIME_MTD projection: (Inner join)

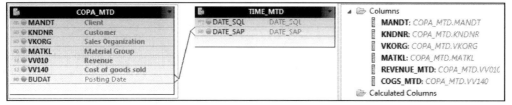

Union both the joins to merge the records of YTD and MTD:

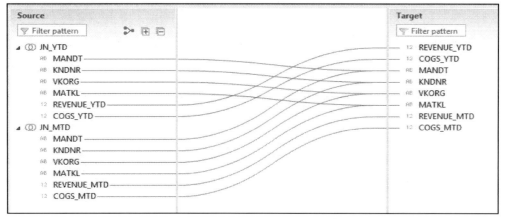

Note: Observe the target fields and mappings and implement in the same manner. In this union node we have to map the attributes from both the sources and measures from only the respective sources

Final Aggregation Node:

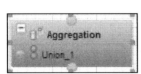
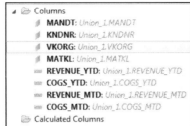

Final step: Activate the Calculation View and verify the activation job log.

1. Verify the output of calculation view
Open the Data Preview for calculation view and enter the value for Input parameter as shown below.

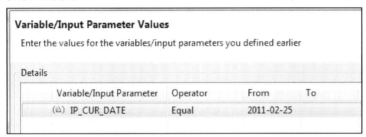

- Result of the calculation view: verify the results of YTD and MTD measures

KNDNR	VKORG	MATKL	REVENUE_YTD	COGS_YTD	REVENUE_MTD	COGS_MTD
COL107	3000	00207	73,218.86	61,732.97	73,218.86	61,732.97
COL108	3000	00207	9,456	7,245.77	9,456	7,245.77
COL106	3000	00207	23,091.43	17,031.94	23,091.43	17,031.94
COL101	3000	00207	72,209.15	49,539.15	72,209.15	49,539.15

- Validate the results by comparing the data in the source table - VBAK
  Query for YTD results:

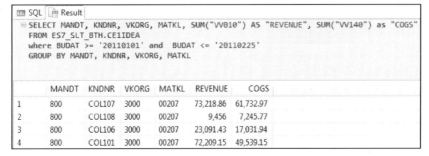

3.6.6 Business Case: Open Purchase Orders Reporting

Requirement: An organization would like to analyze the Open PO (Purchase Order) Count and Open PO Quantities. To achieve this, for each Purchase Order item we need to compare the Purchase Order Quantity with the corresponding Goods receipt(GR) quantity. The difference between PO Qty and GR Qty is used to derive the Open PO Qty. For all the Purchase Order items where the Open PO Qty is more than 0, consider them as Open Purchase Order lines.

Key features of the solution include:
- ✓ Calculated Columns - Counts
- ✓ Calculation before Aggregation behavior using Keep Flag

Graphical View and Sample result:

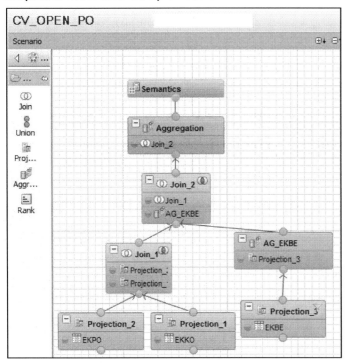

Projection_1: PO Header table fields (EKKO). Apply filtler on BSTYP = F to bring only Purchase orders.

SAP® HANA Modeling Practical World — Calculation Views - Modeling Techniques

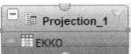
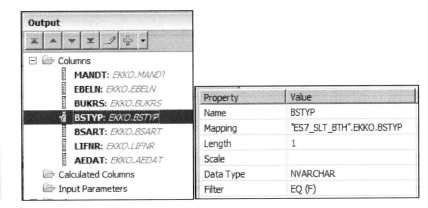

Projection_2: PO Header table fields (EKPO)

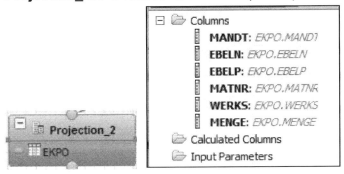

Join_1: Join the PO Header and Items (Join Type: Inner Join)

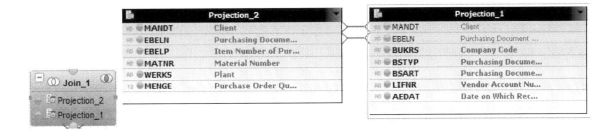

103

Projection_3: Filter on PO History table to bring only Goods Receipts

Filter on the Event Type VGABE = 1 (Goods Receipt)

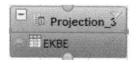

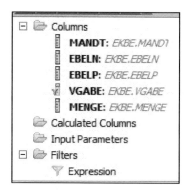
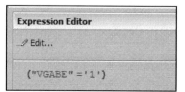

Ag_EKBE: Aggregation of GR Qty for PO History (EKBE) table:

Since there can be multiple Goods receipts for a specific PO Line item, we have to sum up the GR quantity for each PO Line item.

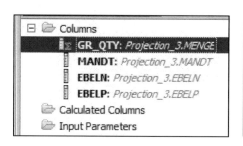

Join 2: To join the PO Line items with the respective PO History entries (Goods Receipt)
Join Type: Left Outer

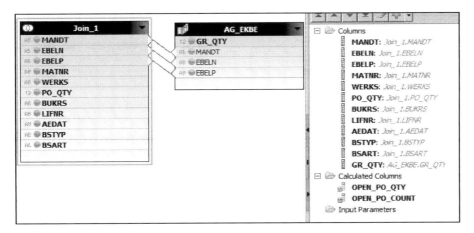

Implement the following calculated columns:

Name	Type	Data type & size	Formula
OPEN_PO_QTY	Measure	Double	"PO_QTY" – "GR_QTY"
OPEN_PO_COUNT	Measure	Integer	If ("OPEN_PO_QTY" > 0, 1, 0)

Final Aggregation:

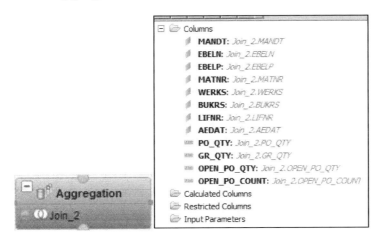

SAP® HANA Modeling Practical World — Calculation Views - Modeling Techniques

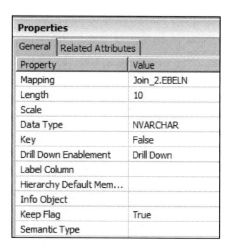

Set the Keep Flag = True for both EBEN and EBELP. This will ensure that the Open PO Quantity is always calculated at the PO Line item level, before the aggregation of the measures.

Maintain Variables:

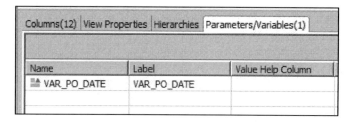

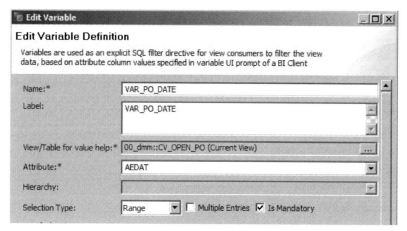

Validate Results:

Below query will show the individual PO line item level Open PO Qty and Count and the results are matching as per the criteria:

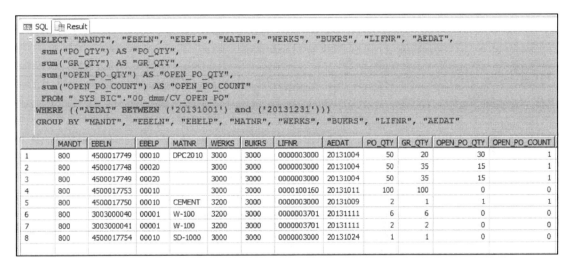

Verify the summary of Open PO Count and Open PO Qty:

```sql
SELECT "MANDT", "WERKS", "BUKRS", "AEDAT",
  sum("PO_QTY") AS "PO_QTY",
  sum("GR_QTY") AS "GR_QTY",
  sum("OPEN_PO_QTY") AS "OPEN_PO_QTY",
  sum("OPEN_PO_COUNT") AS "OPEN_PO_COUNT"
FROM "_SYS_BIC"."00_dmm/CV_OPEN_PO"
WHERE (("AEDAT" BETWEEN ('20131001') and ('20131231')))
GROUP BY "MANDT", "WERKS", "BUKRS", "AEDAT"
```

	MANDT	WERKS	BUKRS	AEDAT	PO_QTY	GR_QTY	OPEN_PO_QTY	OPEN_PO_COUNT
1	800	3000	3000	20131004	150	90	60	3
2	800	3000	3000	20131011	100	100	0	0
3	800	3200	3000	20131009	2	1	1	1
4	800	3200	3000	20131111	8	8	0	0
5	800	3000	3000	20131024	1	1	0	0

4 SQL Script Programming and Applications

Key features of SQL Script:
- SQL Script is the proprietary database programming for SAP HANA, which provides the procedural approach to implement necessary operations and business logic.
- SQLScript allows us to push the data-intensive application logic into the database (Code to Data approach). This approach will help us in optimizing performance of many application areas such as:
    - Native HANA solutions
    - HANA based data mart solutions
    - SAP BW Transformations
    - Planning functions in BW-IP (Integrated Planning)

Traditional DB model -"Data to Code"   **HANA approach "Code to Data"**

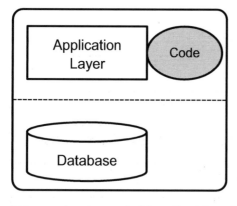 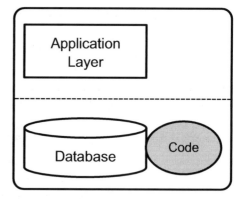

- We can implement side-effect free (Read Only) logic in SQLScript, that operate on tables using SQL queries for set processing and is therefore parallelizable over multiple processors.
- SQL Script also provides various built-in application functions and libraries like::
    - APL (Application Programming Library)
    - PAL (Predictive Analytics Library) and AFL (Application Function Library)

4.1 Key elements of SQL script programming

We can use the following types of processing blocks to implement the solutions using SQL Script, natively in HANA database.

- Stored procedures – Used to perform data access or data manipulation operations

- Scalar Functions – To implement logic for deriving a single column

- Table Functions – To implement logic for deriving a set of records

Typically, the processing logic in SQL script programming involves the steps such as, data retrieval from various tables and views performing calculations and returning the results back to the calling entity.

In the following sections, let us understand the key elements of SQL script programming.

- Data Types and Variables
- Conditional statements (IF, CASE..)
- Looping statements (FOR Loop, While Loop..)
- Scalar and Table Variables
- Built-in functions and User defined functions
- Cursors and Arrays

4.1.1 Data Types and Variables

Below are the pre-defined data types in SQL Script

Classification	Data Type
Date time types	DATE, TIME, SECONDDATE, TIMESTAMP
Numeric types	TINYINT, SMALLINT, INTEGER, BIGINT, DECIMAL, REAL, DOUBLE
Character string types	VARCHAR, NVARCHAR, ALPHANUM, SHORTTEXT
Binary types	VARBINARY
Large Object types	BLOB, CLOB, NCLOB, TEXT
Multi-valued types	ARRAY

HANA Modeling Practical World — SQL Script Programming and Applications

Key Points about Data Types:

- The default format for the **DATE** data type is 'YYYY-MM-DD'

- A character string constant is enclosed in single quotation marks. (eg: 'Test')

- Implicit type conversion: When a given set of operand/argument types does not match what an operator/function expects, a type conversion is carried out by the SAP HANA database.

Types of Variables in HANA:

1) Scalar Variables: These are used to store values of single fields like Customer_Num, Revenue etc..

2) Table Variables: They are used to store group of records in a table strcture

```
Declaring Scalar Variables:
        DECLARE V_CustID NVARCHAR(10)   ;
        DECLARE V_NetValue DECIMAL(15,2)  ;

Assigning Values:
        V_CustID := 'C001'     ;
        V_NetValue := 125.30   ;
        V_NetValue := :V_NetValue  + 100 ;
```

Note:

We have to use := as the assignment operator

To access the variable, we must use :<Variable name> as shown in the example above.

Comments in the code:

Single line comments will be denoted using --

Multi-line comments will be denoted using /*   */

4.1.2 Table Variables

Table variables are used to hold the data records during the runtime of a program. We can fetch the data from any table or view into a table variable. Also, we can run a query (SELECT only) against a table variable in the similar way we run on a table or view. Due to these functionalities, table variables are the most widely used objects in the processing blocks of SQL Script.

Declaring a Table variable:

There are different ways to define the structure for table variables as explained below.

- Automatic generation of table variables based on SQL query

  ```
  TAB_MATERIAL = SELECT MATNR, MTART, MATKL from MARA;
  ```

  In this method the structure of table variable will be generated based on the fields of the SQL query. This is a great flexibility in SQL Script since we don't need to declare the data type for the table variable.

- Definition of Table variable structure locally

- Definition of Table variable structure globally using table types

Fetching records into table variable

We can add the records into a table variable only by using the SELECT statement. Table variables do not support any Data Manipulations such as INSERT, UPDATE, DELETE since these are not persisting the results in the database.

```
SALES_TAB = SELECT VBAP.MANDT, VBAP.VBELN, VBAP.POSNR,VBAP.VGBEL,
VBAP.VGPOS,
          VBAK.ERDAT, VBAK.NETWR
          from VBAP  INNER JOIN VBAK
          ON VBAP.VBELN = VBAK.VBELN;
```

| HANA Modeling Practical World | SQL Script Programming and Applications |

Fetching records from table variables

We need to use the SELECT statement to fetch the record from Table Variables.

Note: We need to address the Table variables also with the prefix : (Colon)

In the below example we are populating the records in the table variable DEL_TAB by reading from another table variable SALES_TAB.

```
DEL_TAB =
   SELECT S.*,LIPS.VBELN AS LIPSVBELN FROM :SALES_TAB AS S
      INNER JOIN LIPS
      ON S.VBELN = LIPS.VGBEL AND S.POSNR = LIPS.VGPOS;
```

Note: Since we cannot run any data manipulation statements like INSERT, UPDATE on the table variables, we need to use the following approaches to achieve the similar functionality.

Merging or Appending records into Table Variables

We can use the UNION operation:

1) To append new records to a table variable without clearing the existing records:

```
TAB_RESULT = SELECT * FROM :TAB_RESULT
               UNION ALL
               SELECT * from :OPEN_ORDER_TAB;
```

2) To merge records from multiple sources into one table variable

```
-- Open & Closed order information is merged.
TAB_RESULT = SELECT * FROM :OPEN_ORDER_TAB
               UNION ALL
               SELECT * FROM :CLOSED_ORDER_TAB;
```

Updating records of Table Variables

We can use the SELECT statement in the following way to update the records within a table variable.

For example, we need to increase the Sales Revenue by 100 for all the Sales orders of a specific Customer:

```
TAB_SALES  = SELECT VBELN, KUNNR, NETWR + 100 as NETWR
             From :TAB_SALES
             Where KUNNR = '10000011';
```

Deleting records from Table Variables

For example, we need to delete the records from table variable where the Sales orders net value is below 1000:

```
TAB_SALES  = SELECT * From :TAB_SALES
             Where NETWR >= 1000;
```

| SAP® HANA Modeling Practical World | SQL Script Programming and Applications |

4.1.3 Built-in Functions in SQL Script

Following are some of the built-in functions in SQL Script, which can be used to perform some of the common operations. These standard functions will help us greatly in implementing the logic in SQL script

Type of Function	Function names
Data Type Conversion	CAST, TO_DATE, TO_VARCHAR, TO_DECIMAL..
Date Time Functions	CURRENT_DATE, DAYS_BETWEEN, ADD_DAYS, ADD_MONTHS, DAYNAME, EXTRACT..
Number Functions	ABS, CEIL, EXP, SQRT, COS..
String Functions	SUBSTRING, CONCAT, LEFT, LENGTH, TRIM, REPLACE, RPAD..
Window Functions	To divide the result sets of a query, or a logical partition of a query, into groups of rows called window partitions. Functions: ROW_NUMBER, RANK..
Miscellaneous Functions	IFNULL, SESSION_USER, CURRENT_SCHEMA, CONVERT_CURRENCY

Examples:

SELECT LAST_DAY (TO_DATE('2010-01-04', 'YYYY-MM-DD')) "last day" FROM DUMMY;

SELECT ADD_MONTHS (TO_DATE ('2009-12-05', 'YYYY-MM-DD'), 1) "add months" FROM DUMMY;

SELECT CAST (10.5 AS INTEGER) "cast" FROM DUMMY;

SELECT IFNULL ('diff', 'same') "ifnull" FROM DUMMY;

Note: DUMMY is a pseudo table in SAP HANA database, which does not have any structure. Hence it can be used to run a query to derive one of more columns with the required functionality.

114

4.1.4 Cursors - operations for looping on data records

Cursors are used to fetch the records sequentially from a table or view and process these records inside a loop. Cursors are ideally used in the scenarios where we need to perform record level operations.

Note: Avoid using Cursors are larger data sets, since they are usually inefficient due to the row by row access to the database tables.

Declare Cursor Variable:

DECLARE **C_VBAK** FOR

SELECT VBELN, KUNNR, NETWR FROM VBAK WHERE VBTYP = 'C'

Steps to process the records using Cursors:

- Open Cursor (Declaring Cursor variable which is always linked to the respective SELECT query)

- Fetch records using cursor variable

- Close the Cursor variable

We can perform the record by record processing of Cursors in two ways.

1) Explicit Looping: Using OPEN Cursor, FETCH records using a WHILE Loop and CLOSE the cursor
2) Implicit Loop on Cursor variable: Using the FOR loop on Cursor variable
   This is commonly used since it performs the Open / Fetch and Close operations implicitly

Open the Cursor:

OPEN CURSOR C_VBAK;

Fetch data records using Cursor:

FETCH C_VBAK into :V_VBELN, :V_KUNNR, :V_NETWR;

Closing Cursor:

CLOSE CURSOR C_VBAK;

SAP® HANA Modeling	SQL Script Programming and Applications
Practical World	

Implicit processing of Cursor variables:

To open a cursor variable that has been defined in the program and to iterate over the result set of the query we can use the FOR loop as shown below.

```
FOR <ROW_VARIABLE>  as <CURSOR> (<optional arguments>) DO
--Processing logic for row wise operations
END FOR ;
```

Example:

```
FOR REC_VBAK as C_VBAK    DO
--Processing logic for row wise operations
END FOR ;
```

Deriving properties of Cursor variables:

Each cursor variable will have the following built-in attributes which can be accessed as per our need.

<Cursor_variable>::IS_CLOSED → To check if a cursor variable is closed

This can be used to ensure that the Cursor variable is currently closed, before trying to perform OPEN Cursor or FOR Loop on this. This will help us to avoid this exception

<Cursor_variable>::ROW_COUNT→ To check the number of rows in the result set of the query attached to the cursor variable

<Cursor_variable>::NOTFOUND → To check if the previous FETCH operation is successful either explicitly or implicitly during the processing in FOR loop

116

SAP® HANA Modeling Practical World	SQL Script Programming and Ap

4.1.5 Arrays and their application for complex calculations

In SQL Script we normally prefer table variables to process group of records. However, table variables do not support record by record processing. Especially in the scenarios where we need to refer to the values from another record in the same set, it will not be possible with table variables while accessing them in SELECT statement. This is where we can leverage the Arrays.

An array is a variable of type ARRAY, which can store a group of elements of same data type. In that sense an array represents a single column. By defining multiple arrays that represents a group of columns we can achieve tabular data processing, where a group of data records are processed sequentially.

Possible operations on arrays
- Built set of elements
- Fetch the values of specific elements
- Merge data of two arrays
- Transferring data from Arrays into a table variable
- Moving data from table variable into arrays
- Looping through the array elements
- Clear the memory for array

Declare Array for storing data
- You could use any primitive data types of SQL script.
- If we use DECIMAL type in array and try to read its value will lead to a compile error. In such cases we need to use DOUBLE data type and convert it back to decimal if needed.

Example:

DECLARE A_KUNNR TYPE NVARCHAR(10) ARRAY;
DECLARE A_NETWR DOUBLE ARRAY;

Fill arrays with values
We can assign the values to the elements using an index notation, which starts from 1.
Example: A_KUNNR[1] = '1001';

Fill arrays with values from a table variable
After binding a select statement to a table variable, using ARRAY_AGG command to fill column data into array
- Sort data by primary key to ensure each array have the same order, then we could use one index to access fields of same record

117

SAP® HANA Modeling Practical World · SQL Script Programming and Applications

- Data types of array element and table column must be same

Example:

```
TAB_SALES = SELECT KUNNR, SUM(NETWR) from VBAK where VBTYP = 'C' GROUP
BY KUNNR;

A_KUNNR := ARRAY_AGG(:TAB_SALES.KUNNR ORDER BY "KUNNR");
A_NETWR := ARRAY_AGG(:TAB_SALES.NETWR ORDER BY "KUNNR");
```

Loop over data from or set value to the array
- We can use FOR Loop to process the array elements in a sequence
- Use the CARDINALITY function to get the number of elements in an array

```
FOR V_INDEX IN 1 .. CARDINALITY(:A_KUNNR) DO
        IF ( :A_NETWR[:V_INDEX] = 0 );
                ELSE
        END IF;
END FOR;
```

Combine arrays to a table variable
Using UNNEST command to combine arrays to a table variable
Example:
TAB_SALES = UNNEST(:A_KUNNR, :A_NETWR);

Removing the elements of Arrays
We can use the TRIM_ARRAY function to remove the given number of elements at the end of the array.

If we want to remove all the elements in an array (i.e. to clean up the array) we can use the CARDINALITY function that will return the total number of elements in an array.

Examples:

TRIM_ARRAY(:A_KUNNR, 1);

TRIM_ARRAY(:A_KUNNR, CARDINALITY(:A_KUNNR));

Example for Arrays: Business Case: Derive Validity Dates for Routing Task Lists

118

| SAP® HANA Modeling | SQL Script Programming and Ap |
| Practical World | |

4.1.6 Exception Handling Techniques

Due to multiple reasons, statements in SQL Script programs can be terminated since the system cannot handle those situations. For example: Arithmetic overflow, Divide by Zero error. These are considered as system defined exceptions.

We can also implement user defined exceptions, that will allow us to implement the actions (such as generating error messages) to handle specific scenarios in the business logic. For example, if we want to generate an exception when the user entry for Start Date is later than End Date.

Hence it is important to add the exception handling logic to build robust programs. SQL Script provides the following statement to handle the exceptions.

- The DECLARE EXIT HANDLER statement allows you to define exception handlers to process exception conditions in your procedures.

- You use the DECLARE CONDITION parameter to name exception conditions, and optionally, their associated SQL state values.

- You can use SIGNAL or RESIGNAL with specified error code in user-defined error code range. A user-defined exception can be handled by the handler declared in the procedure. Also, it can be handled by the caller which can be another procedure or client.

4.1.7 Scalar Functions

Scalar Functions allow us to implement a reusable logic that returns a single value. For example, we can build a scalar function (named IS_NUMERIC) that can check if the given value is a numeric and return the values 0 (False) or 1 (True).

Key features of Scalar Functions:
- Can have any number of input parameters
- Expression statements are allowed within the body
- Table operations such as CURSOR, CE functions or Array operations are not allowed
- Input parameters used in the signature of scalar function cannot be of "Table Type"

Steps to implement Scalar Functions:
- We can create scalar functions in the HANA Development perspective.
- There are created using the extension .hdbscalarfunction

Options to Consume Scalar Functions:
- Scalar functions can be consumed from the field list or the WHERE clause of the SELECT statement.
- We can also use them to derive the values for Input Parameters
- They can be also used for direct assignment into variables: Example Var1 := scalar_function()

SAP® HANA Modeling Practical World	SQL Script Programming and

Example: Following Scalar function will return the date in external format

```
FUNCTION "NVARMA"."VDEMO1::SAPDATE_TO_EXTDATE" ( I_DATE
VARCHAR(8))
      RETURNS O_DATE nvarchar(10)
      LANGUAGE SQLSCRIPT
      SQL SECURITY INVOKER AS
BEGIN
--YYYYMMDD to DD-MM-YYYY

DECLARE lv_datemonth VARCHAR(6);

SELECT concat(CONCAT(substr(i_date,7,2),'-') ,
      concat(substr(i_date,5,2),'-'))
      INTO lv_datemonth from dummy;

SELECT concat(lv_datemonth ,substr(i_date,1,4)) into O_DATE from
dummy;
END;
```

This is how we can consume a scalar function from a SQL statement: Here we are deriving a field using the scalar function.

```
select "NVARMA"."VDEMO1::SAPDATE_TO_EXTDATE"('20180210') from dummy
```

	NVARMA.VDEMO1::SAPDATE_TO_EXTDATE('20180210')	
1	10-02-2018	

| ® HANA Modeling Practical World | SQL Script Programming and Applications |

4.2 Table Functions

Table Functions are used to implement the solutions where we need to return the results represented in a table. Mostly we will implement table functions to address the data modeling requirements which canot be achieved using graphical calculation views.

Key features of Table Functions:
- Replaces the Script based Calculation views
- Can be used as data sources in graphical calculation views
- Read-only – we cannot implement any logic that updates the data
- Accept multiple input parameters and return exactly one results table

Key Points:
- Watch out for the performance while integrating the Table functions in Calculation views
- We can pass the values from Calculation views to Table functions using Input Parameters mapping technique

Options to Consume Scalar Functions:
- We can use the table functions as data source in calculation views
- We can call the table functions from stored procedures and other table functions

Syntax: Table Function definition

```
FUNCTION <Name> ( <Input Parameters>)
     RETURNS TABLE ( <Table fields>)
     LANGUAGE SQLSCRIPT
     SQL SECURITY INVOKER AS
BEGIN

<Processing Logic>
RETURN <Select statement with the list of Output columns>
END;
```

Example for Table Function: Practical Solutions and Examples Using SQL script (End of this unit)

122

4.3 Stored procedures

Stored procedures are the reusable processing blocks of logic, which can be used to implement solutions as per specific business requirements.

Commonly we implement stored procedures to build the solutions for the scenarios such as:

1) Persisting results in HANA database – example Snapshots, Reusable results of HANA views – to avoid frequent execution of complex views.
2) Reusable solutions – Data conversions, Calculations etc.

- Procedures can be defined as Read only OR Read / Write Procedures
- These are the typical ways of calling procedures:
    - Calling stored procedures from another procedure or function
    - Scheduling the procedure call from XS Job engine which is in-build in HANA
    - Scheduling the procedure call from external ETL tools such as Business Objects Data Services

Procedures can be created as:

1. Catalog Procedures: These are not transportable, since they are created using the CREATE PROCEDURE statement and they are not created under a package.
2. Repository Procedures: These are the procedures created using the HANA development perspective (Extension .hdbprocedure). This is the recommended approach for creating stored procedures since they can be transported, and version management is available

| SAP® HANA Modeling Practical World | SQL Script Programming and Applications |

Stored Procedure Syntax:

Definition of procedure:

```
PROCEDURE <Name> (Parameters)
      LANGUAGE SQLSCRIPT
      SQL SECURITY INVOKER
      DEFAULT SCHEMA <SCHEMA>
      READ ONLY
       AS
BEGIN
      --- Processing Block----

END;
```

Calling Procedure:

```
CALL <Procedure Name> (<Actual Parameters>);
```

Parameter types:

IN: These are passed as input values to the procedure

OUT: They will act as return values from the procedure

INOUT: These are a combination of both the above – acts both as and input and return values

We can use both Scalar variables and Table Variables as the parameters for stored procedures.

124

4.3.1 Real time reporting vs Persisted results

One of the key decision criteria that we normally come across in the HANA modeling solutions is whether to implement the information view to enable real time reporting (on the fly calculations) or to implement it based on the persisted results, which are stored in a custom table in HANA. This custom table will be updated using a stored procedure.

Which are the ideal scenarios to implement Persistence based solutions?
- Some of the highly processing intensive calculations where the real time reporting is not essential
- The scenarios like calculating and storing snapshots of results (such as weekly inventory snapshots)

Solution Approach: Implement the logic using Procedures in HANA to persist the results in a table. Subsequently a calculation view can be built on this table to enable reporting.

Persistence Based Solutions: Solution Approach Diagram:

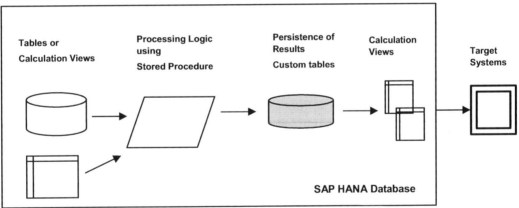

Advantages:

- Allows us build historical truth-based reporting solutions in HANA such as Snapshots
- Optimal system performance by avoiding repeated execution of complex logic

Disadvantages:

- Does not provide real time reporting
- Need for additional storage in HANA due to the persistence of results

4.3.2 Best Practices in SQL Script:

- Try to minimize the data transferred by using appropriate WHERE conditions, Field lists, and Aggregations in the queries.

  Avoid using SELECT *, since it will fetch all the columns from the table. Column store operations should be restricted to only necessary columns to achieve better performance

- Adopt proper naming standards for the various elements such as Table Variables, Local variables, Arrays, Cursors etc.

- Suggested methods while performing operations on group of records:

  - To process a group of records from set of tables, where there is no need of addressing specific record – use Table Variables
  - To process the records sequentially inside a loop – Use Cursors. However, cursors will affect the performance when large number of records are processed
  - To access a different record in the same dataset while processing a group of records – use Arrays.

- If you split a complex query into logical sub queries it can help the optimizer to identify common sub expressions and to derive more efficient execution plans.

- Insert a set of data records into the database because a single unit is much more efficient than inserting the records one by one

- Implement exception handling to ensure there won't be any run time errors such as "Numeric Overflow" during the execution

- Executing dynamic SQL is slow because compile time checks and query optimization must be done for every invocation of the procedure

| SAP® HANA Modeling Practical World | SQL Script Programming and Applications |

4.4 Practical Solutions and Examples Using SQL script

Let us go through few examples and scenarios where we can build solutions using SQL Script programming. Try to understand the application of various elements of SQL script programming.

4.4.1 Business Case: Derive Validity Dates for Routing Task Lists

Implement the following reporting logic based on SAP Routing Task List (PLKO table). In this example we have created a similar table names as TASKLIST_HDR.

This table has the header details from task lists. It has a Valid-From date from each task list. However, it does not have the Valid-To date. As part of this requirement we need to derive the Valid-To date based on the Valid-From date of the previous entry in the task list.

Key Learnings:
- Processing data using Table variables
- Usage of Arrays
- Implementing Scalar Functions
- Building Table functions

Solution Details:

Calculation logic for the VALID_TO date for each of the Task List header entries.

- If the next record belongs to the same Task List group set the VALID_TO of current record
  as the VALID_FROM Minus 1, of the next record
- ELSE set the VALID_TO as '9999-12-31'

Let us see how we can achieve this requirement by using the Arrays.

Step 1: Create the following table like the task list table above: TASKLIST_HDR

Note: This table is similar to SAP Standard Table: PLKO (Task List Header)

127

```
select * from nvarma.TASKLIST_HDR
```

	TASKLIST_TYPE	TASKLIST_GROUP	GROUP_COUNTER	INTERNAL_COUNTER	VALID_FROM
1	R	GRP001	C1	001	Jan 1, 2017
2	R	GRP001	C1	002	Mar 1, 2017
3	R	GRP001	C1	003	May 10, 2017
4	R	GRP002	X1	001	Jan 1, 2018
5	R	GRP002	X1	002	Feb 1, 2018
6	R	GRP002	X1	003	Apr 15, 2018

Step 2: Implement the following Table Function to build the logic to derive "Valid To Date" for each of the Task List entries.

```
FUNCTION "NVARMA"."00_dmm::TASK_LIST_VALIDITY" ( )
     RETURNS TABLE (

                         TASKLIST_TYPE NVARCHAR(1),
                         TASKLIST_GROUP  NVARCHAR(8),
                         GROUP_COUNTER NVARCHAR(2),
                         INTERNAL_COUNTER NVARCHAR(3),
                         VALID_FROM DATE,
                         VALID_TO DATE)


     LANGUAGE SQLSCRIPT
     SQL SECURITY INVOKER AS
BEGIN
/****************************
     Write your function logic
 ****************************/
DECLARE A_TASKLIST_TYPE NVARCHAR(1) ARRAY;
DECLARE A_TASKLIST_GROUP NVARCHAR(8) ARRAY;
DECLARE A_GROUP_COUNTER NVARCHAR(2) ARRAY;
DECLARE A_INTERNAL_COUNTER NVARCHAR(3) ARRAY;
DECLARE A_VALID_FROM DATE ARRAY;
DECLARE A_VALID_TO DATE ARRAY;

DECLARE V_INDEX INTEGER;
DECLARE V_NEXT INTEGER;
```

--Fetch the Task list entries from database table into table variable

```
TAB_TASKLIST =      SELECT
                                    "TASKLIST_TYPE",
                                    "TASKLIST_GROUP",
                                    "GROUP_COUNTER",
                                    "INTERNAL_COUNTER" ,
                                    "VALID_FROM"
                    from nvarma.TASKLIST_HDR        ;
```

--Fill the arrays from the respective columns of table variable

```
A_TASKLIST_TYPE := ARRAY_AGG(:TAB_TASKLIST.TASKLIST_TYPE
                ORDER BY "TASKLIST_TYPE","TASKLIST_GROUP","GROUP_COUNTER",
                "INTERNAL_COUNTER");
A_TASKLIST_GROUP := ARRAY_AGG(:TAB_TASKLIST.TASKLIST_GROUP
                ORDER BY "TASKLIST_TYPE","TASKLIST_GROUP","GROUP_COUNTER",
                "INTERNAL_COUNTER");
A_GROUP_COUNTER := ARRAY_AGG(:TAB_TASKLIST.GROUP_COUNTER
                ORDER BY "TASKLIST_TYPE","TASKLIST_GROUP","GROUP_COUNTER",
                "INTERNAL_COUNTER");
A_INTERNAL_COUNTER := ARRAY_AGG(:TAB_TASKLIST.INTERNAL_COUNTER
                ORDER BY "TASKLIST_TYPE","TASKLIST_GROUP","GROUP_COUNTER",
                "INTERNAL_COUNTER");
A_VALID_FROM := ARRAY_AGG(:TAB_TASKLIST.VALID_FROM
                ORDER BY "TASKLIST_TYPE","TASKLIST_GROUP","GROUP_COUNTER",
                "INTERNAL_COUNTER");
```

--Loop through the Arrays to determine the VALID_TO date based on the VALID_FROM date --of the next record

```
FOR V_INDEX IN 1 .. CARDINALITY(:A_TASKLIST_GROUP) DO

        V_NEXT := V_INDEX + 1;
```

-- If the next record belongs to the same Task List group set the
-- VALID_TO of current record as the VALID_FROM minus 1 of the
-- next record ELSE set it as '9999-12-31'

```
if ( :A_TASKLIST_TYPE[:V_NEXT] = :A_TASKLIST_TYPE[:V_INDEX] AND
      :A_TASKLIST_GROUP[:V_NEXT] = :A_TASKLIST_GROUP[:V_INDEX] AND
      :A_GROUP_COUNTER[:V_NEXT] = :A_GROUP_COUNTER[:V_INDEX]) THEN

A_VALID_TO[:V_INDEX] := ADD_DAYS(:A_VALID_FROM[:V_NEXT], -1);

        ELSE
A_VALID_TO[:V_INDEX] := TO_DATE ('9999-12-31', 'YYYY-MM-DD');
```

```
        END IF;

END FOR;
```

--Transfer the results from Arrays into another table variable

```
TAB_RESULT = UNNEST( :A_TASKLIST_TYPE,  :A_TASKLIST_GROUP,
:A_GROUP_COUNTER, :A_INTERNAL_COUNTER, :A_VALID_FROM, :A_VALID_TO)
              AS (TASKLIST_TYPE, TASKLIST_GROUP, GROUP_COUNTER,
INTERNAL_COUNTER , VALID_FROM, VALID_TO);
```

--Return the results from table function

```
        RETURN SELECT * from :TAB_RESULT;

END;
```

Results of Table Function:

Execute the following query on the table function and validate the results

SQL | Result

```
select * from "NVARMA"."00_dmm::TASK_LIST_VALIDITY"()
```

	TASKLIST_TYPE	TASKLIST_GROUP	GROUP_COUNTER	INTERNAL_COUNTER	VALID_FROM	VALID_TO
1	R	GRP001	C1	001	Jan 1, 2017	Feb 28, 2017
2	R	GRP001	C1	002	Mar 1, 2017	May 9, 2017
3	R	GRP001	C1	003	May 10, 2017	Dec 31, 9999
4	R	GRP002	X1	001	Jan 1, 2018	Jan 31, 2018
5	R	GRP002	X1	002	Feb 1, 2018	Apr 14, 2018
6	R	GRP002	X1	003	Apr 15, 2018	Dec 31, 9999

Note: Verify the values for VALID_TO in the above result set and notice that these are shown as per the details given in the requirement.

5 HANA Modeling Practical Case studies

Implementing Solutions using Graphical Calculation Views

Learning becomes more interesting when we apply the concepts and implement solutions to address the real-world problems. In this unit, we will go through some of the case studies based on project requirements and learn the solution approaches to build graphical calculation views.

5.1 Business Case: Build Calculation view for Inventory Cycle Count

Requirement description: A company would like to analyze the "physical inventory count completion percentage", which is also known as "Inventory Cycle Count" for a given plant and a date (i.e. as on date). It is essential to have accuracy of Inventory cycle count to have better visibility of material stocks which reflects in the financial statements as well.

Calculation logic for "Inventory count completion percentage":

Total number of materials counted / Actual number of weeks as on current date] / [Total number materials / XX (in this example XX is taken as 12 - number of periods in a year)].

Below are the source tables and sample data:

```
Definition of table: MAT_PLANT
table.schemaName = "NVARMA";
table.tableType = COLUMNSTORE;
table.columns = [
{name = "PLANT"; sqlType = NVARCHAR; length = 4;},
{name = "MATERIAL"; sqlType = NVARCHAR; length = 10;},
{name = "MTYPE"; sqlType = NVARCHAR; length = 10;}] ;

table.primaryKey.pkcolumns = ["PLANT", "MATERIAL"];
```

Contents of table: MAT_PLANT

PLANT ▲	MATERIAL	MTYPE
P001	M1	ROH
P001	M2	ROH
P001	M3	ROH
P001	M4	HALB
P001	M5	HALB
P001	M6	ROH
P001	M7	ROH
P001	M8	ROH
P001	M9	HALB
P001	M10	HALB
P001	M11	ROH
P001	M12	ROH
P001	M13	ROH
P001	M15	ROH
P001	M16	ROH
P001	M14	HALB
P001	M18	ROH
P001	M19	ROH
P001	M20	ROH
P001	M21	ROH
P001	M17	HALB
P001	M22	ROH
P001	M23	ROH
P001	M24	ROH
P002	M1	ROH

Definition of table: INVENTORY_DOC

```
table.schemaName = "NVARMA";
table.tableType = COLUMNSTORE;
table.columns = [
{name = "PLANT"; sqlType = NVARCHAR; length = 4;},
{name = "MATERIAL"; sqlType = NVARCHAR; length = 10;},
{name = "INV_DOC"; sqlType = NVARCHAR; length = 10;},
{name = "DOC_DATE"; sqlType = DATE; },
{name = "QUANTITY"; sqlType = DECIMAL;  precision = 4;}
] ;
table.primaryKey.pkcolumns = ["INV_DOC"];
```

SAP® HANA Modeling Practical World

HANA Modeling Practical Case studies

Table: INVENTORY_DOC

PLANT	MATERIAL	INV_DOC	DOC_DATE	QUANTITY
P001	M1	1000001	Jan 5, 2016	250
P001	M2	1000003	Feb 9, 2016	500
P001	M3	1000004	Feb 25, 2016	300
P001	M4	1000006	Mar 5, 2016	100
P001	M5	1000007	Mar 19, 2016	400
P002	M1	1000002	Jan 11, 2016	150
P002	M3	1000005	Feb 25, 2016	200

Logic to be used for calculation of cycle count completed percentage

A. Based on the user input, select all materials for the given plants. Get the distinct material count in each plant (Table MAT_PLANT). Divide this number for each plant by X (where X = number of periods in a year) to determine the number of materials expected to be counted per period.

> Sample user input: Plant = P001 and Date To = 2016-02-28
>
> Distinct material count for this plant (Table MAT_PLANT) = 24 **(R1)**
>
> No of periods in a year = 12 (We are assuming this for simplification)
>
> Number of materials expected to be counter per period = 24/12 = 2 **(R2)**

B. Use the above list of plant / material data to check how many of these plant materials have been counted at least from the start of the current year till the 'To date' mentioned in the selection screen. Get the distinct count of all such materials in individual plants (Table INVENTORY_DOC).

> No of distinct materials counted in each plant as on the input date in that year
>
> (Table INVENTORY_DOC) = 3 **(R3)**

C. Calculate the "number of periods" from the start of the year till date

> Number of periods as on input date = 2 **(R4)**

D. Get the actual number of materials counted per week by dividing the "plant material count" from step B by "number of weeks" from step C.

> Number of materials expected to be counted = 2 * 2 = 4 **(R5)**

E. Display "actual number of materials counted" (data from step D) as a percentage of "number of materials to be counted" per week (data from step A) for every plant.

> % of materials for which inventory is counted = 3 /4 * 100 = 75%
>
> This is the final value expected for this KPI **(R6)**

Solution Implementation:

Let us approach the solution design for this KPI using the graphical calculation views and leveraging the key features such as input parameters, counters and calculated columns, aggregation, project and join nodes. Further we will try to implement the solution using stacked calculation view approach for better modularization and reusability of views.

Create the following calculation views:

1. CA_MAT_PLANT: To derive the count of materials for a given plant from MAT_PLANT table
2. CA_INV_DOC: To derive the count of distinct plant / materials from the INVENTORY_DOC table
3. CA_INVCOUNT_COMPLETION (Reporting view): Calculate the percentage of materials for which inventory count has been completed as on given date selection for the given plant(s)

Graphical calculation view: CA_MAT_PLANT

Implement this calculation view based on the MAT_PLANT table, and create a "Counter" measure to derive the distinct count of Material & Plant.

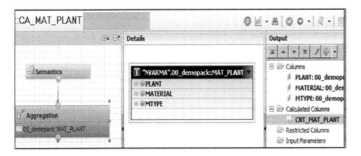
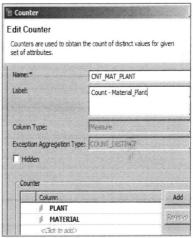

Maintain Semantics:

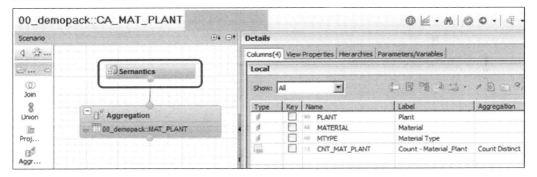

Verify the output of CA_MAT_PLANT using Date Preview:

135

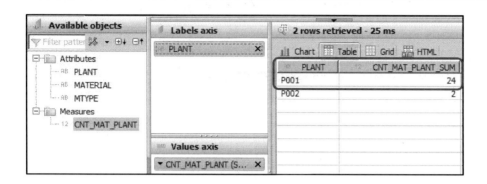

Note: Count of Materials in Plant P001 is 24, which is matching with the expected result **R1**

Calculation view: CA_INV_DOC

Implement this calculation view based on the INVENTORY_DOC table and the CA_MAT_PLANT calculation view

Below is the overall layout of the calculation view:

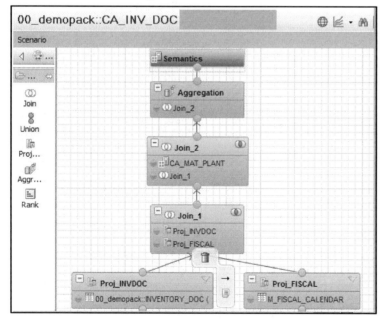

Let us go through the definition of each node:

Node 1: Proj_INVDOC (Projection on table INVENTORY_DOC)

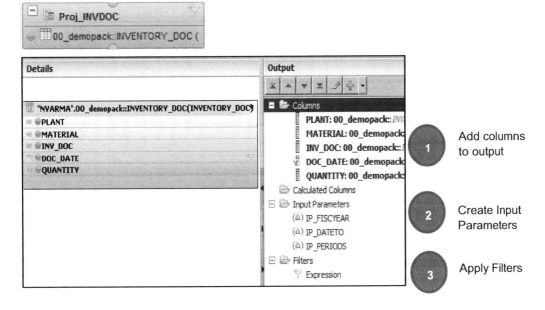

Create the following input parameters:
IP_DATETO
IP_FISCYEAR
IP_PERIODS

| SAP® HANA Modeling Practical World | HANA Modeling Practical Case studies |

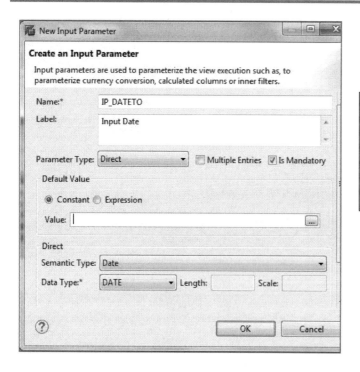

- Input Parameter for date (User input): IP_DATETO (This is used to filter the inventory documents from the table INVENTORY_DOC

- Input Parameter for fiscal year (Derived from Table) – This is used to restrict the inventory documents for only the current year as per the user input which is provided through IP_DATETO. We are leveraging the Parameter Type "Derived from Table", to derive Fiscal Year from the table M_FISCAL_CALENDAR.

Note: You need to use the appropriate value for CALENDAR_VARIANT in the above-mentioned filter values.

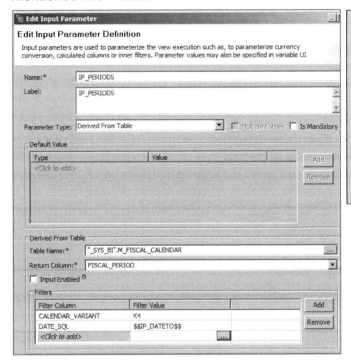

Input Parameter to derive fiscal period (Derived from Table) – This is used to represent the number of periods as per the user input which is provided through IP_DATETO.

We are leveraging the Parameter Type "Derived from Table", to derive Fiscal period from the table M_FISCAL_CALENDAR

Filter expression:

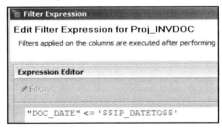

Node 2: Proj_FISCAL(Projection on table M_FISCAL_CALENDAR)

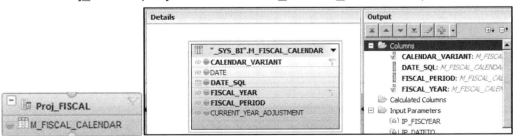

Filter expression: Restrict the Fiscal year variant as applicable and Fiscal year as per the user input date

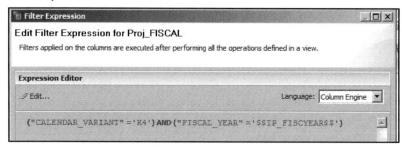

Node 3: Join_1 to join both Proj_INV_DOC and Proj_FISCAL based on document date
Join type: Inner join

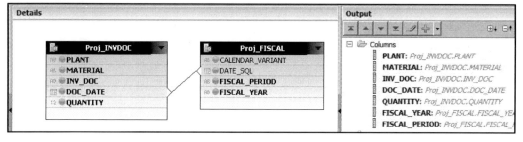

Node 4: Join_2 to join both CA_MAT_PLANT view and Join_1 based on Plant and Material (Join type: Inner join)

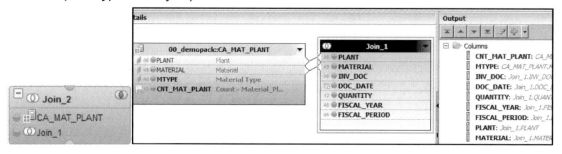

Node 2: Aggregation on the node Join_2, to define the final output structure including a counter measure for Count distinct of Plant and Material

SAP® HANA Modeling Practical World
HANA Modeling Practical Case studies

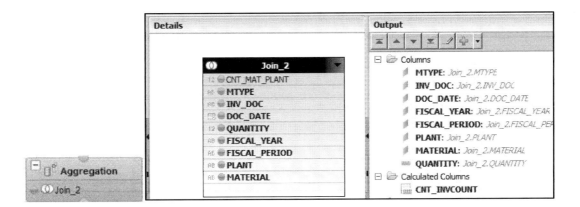

Create the following counter under calculated columns

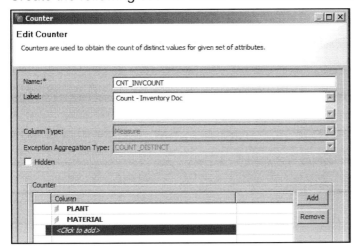

SAP® HANA Modeling Practical World
HANA Modeling Practical Case studies

Maintain the View Semantics: as shown below

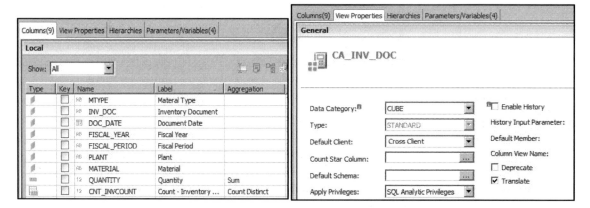

Data Preview:

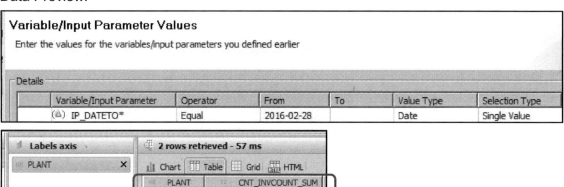

Note: Count of materials with Inventory documents P001 is 3, which is matching with the expected result **R3**

142

Graphical calculation view: CA_INVCOUNT_COMPLETION

Implement this calculation view based on the calculation views CA_INV_DOC and CA_MAT_PLANT

Below is the overall layout of the calculation view:

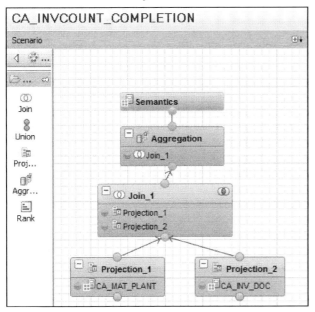

Let us go through the definition of each node:

Node 1: Projection_1 (Projection on the calculation view CA_MAT_PLANT)

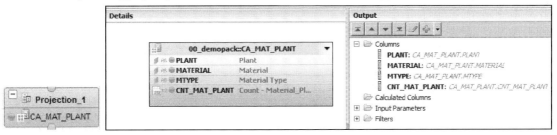

Node 2: Projection_2 (Projection on the calculation view CA_INV_DOC)

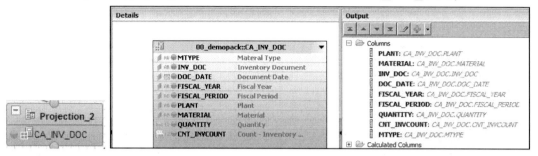

Create Input parameters using the "Manage Mappings" functionality

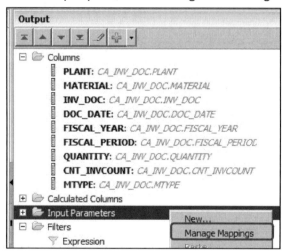

Click on the "Auto map by name" to generate the input parameters automatically and map them with the source views.

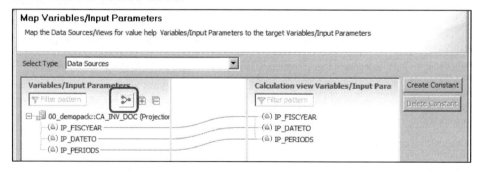

Node 3: Join_1 (Inner join of both the projections of CA_MAT_PLNAT and CA_INV_DOC)
Join type: Inner join

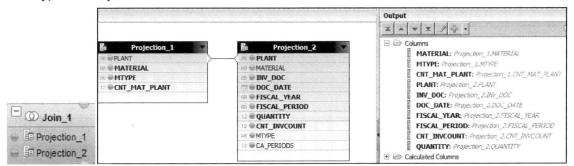

Final Aggregation node as shown below:

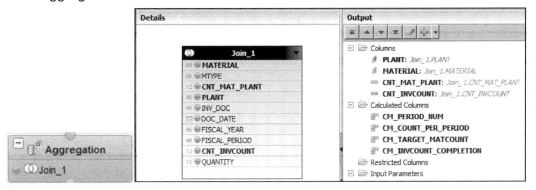

Below are the definitions of the calculated columns

Name	Type	Data Type & Length	Formula
CM_PERIOD_NUM	Measure	Integer	$$IP_PERIODS$$
CM_COUNT_PER_PERIOD	Measure	Decimal (15,2)	Double("CM_MAT_PLNAT"/12)
CM_TARGET_MATCOUNT	Measure	Decimal (15,2)	"CM_COUNT_PER_PERIOD" * "CM_PERIOD_NUM"
CM_INVCOUNT_COMPLETION	Measure	Decimal (15,2)	Double("CNT_INVCOUNT") / Double("CM_TARGET_MATCOUNT") * 100

Main KPI: CM_INVCOUNT_COMPLETION – Set the label as "Inventory Count Completion %"

Semantics of the calculation view: Ensure all the relevant attributes and measures are added as shown below.

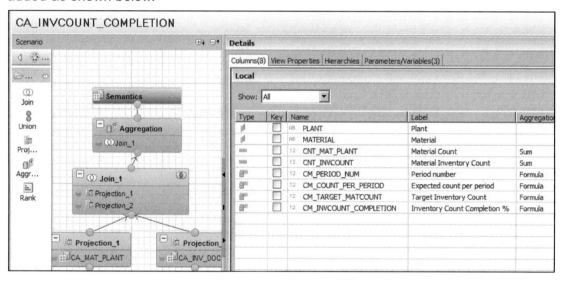

Run the query on calculation view and verify the results:

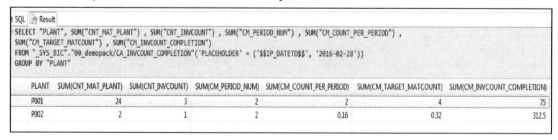

5.2 Business Case: Sales Revenue Percentage Share Calculations

Requirement Description: An organization would like to analyze the "Percentage Share of Sales Revenue" across various dimensions such as Customer, Sales Organization, Distribution Channel, Division etc. for the given periods. As per this requirement we need to implement a Calculation View which provides the flexibility to calculate the Percentage of Share (Revenue) for different combination of dimensions as per the need.

Key concepts:

Dynamic Joins

Aggregation of measures and Calculations

Below is the overall layout of the Calculation view

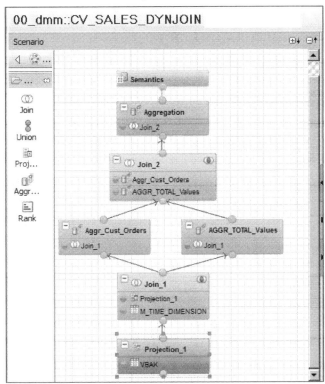

Detailed steps in the calculation view:

Projection_1: Output Columns of Sales Document Header (VBAK Table)

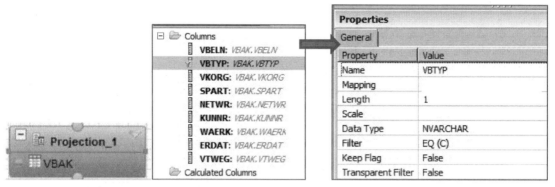

Note: We have applied the filter (VBTYP = 'C') to ensure that only Sales documents of type Sales Orders are fetched from VBAK table

Join_1: Implement join with the Time Dimension (M_TIME_DIMENSION)

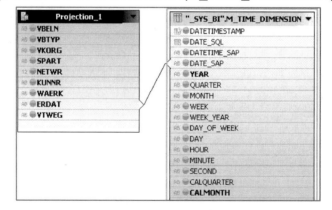

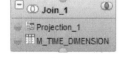

Aggr_Cust_Orders: Aggregate Sales Documents to summarize the Net Value (NETWR)

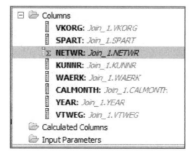

Aggr_TOTAL_Values: This is used to calculate the grand total of Sales Revenue for the given selection of periods

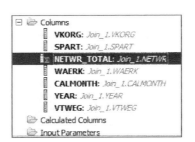
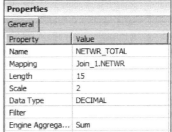

Join_2: Implement "Dynamic join" to perform % Share calculation of Sales Order value

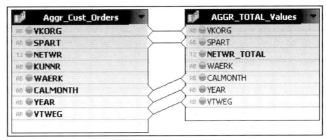

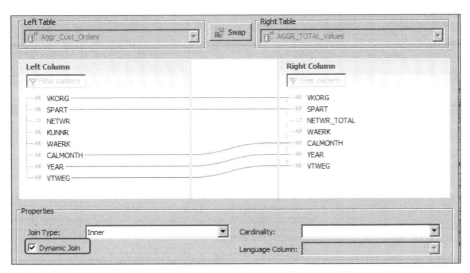

Note: Dynamic join will ensure that the join operation is only performed using those attributes which are requested in the query level.

Implement the Calculated columns to derive the Percentage of Share in Revenue.

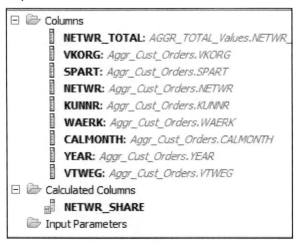

Create the calculated column: NETWR_SHARE

Data Type: Decimal (12,4)

Formula: **if ("NETWR_TOTAL" != 0, double("NETWR")/ "NETWR_TOTAL",0) * 100**

Final Aggregation node: Add the attributes and measures as shown below

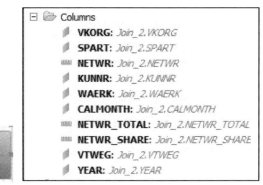

Activate the view and preview the results.

Concept check: We have used the following features to implement the solution:
- ✓ Aggregation nodes – To derive the summary of sales revenue at different levels
- ✓ Dynamic joins – To provide the flexibility to the users for choosing the required attributes where the percentage share of sales revenue can be

150

Below are the sample queries to validate the results:

Case #1: Display the Percentage of share in Revenue (NETWR_SHARE) for each Customer at Sales Organization 3000.

```
SELECT "VKORG","KUNNR", SUM("NETWR"), SUM("NETWR_TOTAL"), SUM("NETWR_SHARE")
    FROM "_SYS_BIC"."00_dmm/CV_SALES_DYNJOIN"
    where "CALMONTH" = '201402' and "VKORG" = '3000'
    GROUP BY "CALMONTH", "VKORG", "KUNNR"
```

SQL | **Result**

```
SELECT "VKORG","KUNNR", SUM("NETWR") , SUM("NETWR_TOTAL") , SUM("NETWR_SHARE")
    FROM "_SYS_BIC"."00_dmm/CV_SALES_DYNJOIN"
    where "CALMONTH" = '201402' and "VKORG" = '3000'
    GROUP BY "CALMONTH", "VKORG", "KUNNR"|
```

	VKORG	KUNNR	SUM(NETWR)	SUM(NETWR_TOTAL)	SUM(NETWR_SHARE)	
1	3000	0000300711	1,000	443,641.42	0.2254	
2	3000	0000003000	183,776	443,641.42	41.4244	
3	3000	0000003001	5,616	443,641.42	1.2658	
4	3000	0000003250	56,000	443,641.42	12.6228	
5	3000	0000500100	197,249.42	443,641.42	44.4614	

Case #2: Display the Percentage of share in Revenue (NETWR_SHARE) for each Distribution channel and Customer at Sales Organization 3000.

```
SELECT  "VKORG","VTWEG", "KUNNR", SUM("NETWR") , SUM("NETWR_TOTAL") ,
SUM("NETWR_SHARE")
FROM "_SYS_BIC"."00_dmm/CV_SALES_DYNJOIN"
where "CALMONTH" = '201402' and "VKORG" = '3000'
GROUP BY "CALMONTH", "VKORG", "VTWEG", "KUNNR"
order by  "VKORG", "VTWEG"
```

SQL | **Result**

```
SELECT "VKORG","VTWEG", "KUNNR", SUM("NETWR") , SUM("NETWR_TOTAL") , SUM("NETWR_SHARE")
    FROM "_SYS_BIC"."00_dmm/CV_SALES_DYNJOIN"
    where "CALMONTH" = '201402' and "VKORG" = '3000'
    GROUP BY "CALMONTH", "VKORG", "VTWEG", "KUNNR"
    order by  "VKORG", "VTWEG"
```

	VKORG	VTWEG	KUNNR	SUM(NETWR)	SUM(NETWR_TOTAL)	SUM(NETWR_SHARE)	
1	3000	10	0000300711	1,000	438,025.42	0.2282	
2	3000	10	0000003000	183,776	438,025.42	41.9555	
3	3000	10	0000003250	56,000	438,025.42	12.7846	
4	3000	10	0000500100	197,249.42	438,025.42	45.0315	
5	3000	12	0000003001	5,616	5,616	100	

| SAP® HANA Modeling | HANA Modeling Practical Case studies |
| Practical World | |

5.3 Business Case: Reporting Month End Inventory Balances of Materials

Requirement Description: An organization would like to report the Month End Inventory Balances for various Materials / Plants for a given Period (Month) based on the following logic:

Note: This case study is based on the SAP standard tables MBEW and MBEWH which contains the inventory values of materials.

A. Get MBEW data for all plant materials: where MBEW-BWTAR = ' ' and MBEW-BWKEY = WERKS (plant from selection screen)

B. Check to see for how many of the materials period (LFGJA and LFMON) matches current period data. Filter out this list from the previous **step A** list.

C. Using the list from **Step B**, fetch data from MBEWH table where MBEWH-MATNR = MATNR from list B, MBEWH-BWKEY = BWKEY for the record from list C, BWTAR = ' ', LFGJA and LFMON will be previous period data. If data is found, then use this data and overwrite the data for these materials in **step A** list. Check to see if data has been retrieved for all materials in list from **step B**.

D. If data has not been retrieved for all materials in **step C** for list from Step C, then get the delta list and fetch data from MBEWH using MATNR and BWKEY for the record, MBEWH-BWTAR = ' ', MBEWH-LFGJA and MBEWH-LFMON will be period prior to the period data used in **step B**. If data is found, then use this data and overwrite the data for these materials in **step A** list. Repeat this (fetching data from MBEWH for previous periods) until previous period data has been fetched for all materials.

E. Once all the data has been fetched, calculate the total value for material (field SALK3) per plant. This is the **Total inventory value** of materials in that plant for the previous period.

Key concepts:

- Left Outer joins for look up operations
- Union Operation for merging the records
- Implementing formulas using Calculated columns and Input Parameters

152

Below are the necessary tables to implement this solution:

Inventory Values for Historical periods (Closed periods)

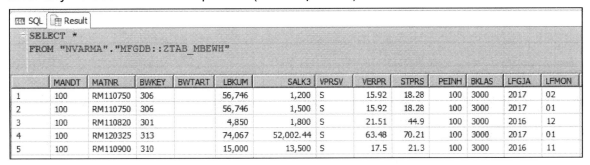

Inventory Values for Current Period

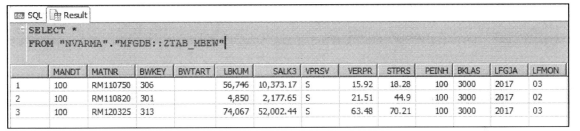

Material Master

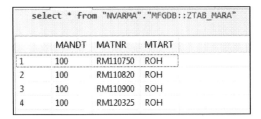

SAP® HANA Modeling Practical World	HANA Modeling Practical Case studies

Logic to be used for Material Month End Balance: Input Date: 2017-03-10 (Closed period 2/2017)

Case #1: Material: RM110750

1. Get the value of stock (SALK3) from MBEW for the given period if exists (10,373.17)
2. Get the value of stock (SALK3) from MBEWH for the latest period which is 2/2017 (1200)
3. The total value of stock will be the addition of the both the above i.e. **11,573.17**

Case #2: Material: RM110820

1. Get the value of stock (SALK3) from MBEW for the previous period if exists (2177.65)
2. No need to read from MBEWH since we found the entry in above step
3. The Closing stock value of material will be from MBEW itself i.e. **2177.65**

Expected result: Column CM_CLOSING_STOCK

MATNR	BKLAS	BWKEY	LBKUM	SALK3	CM_SALK3	CM_FLAG	CM_STK_VAL	CM_CLOSING_STOCK
RM110750	3000	306	113,492	11,573.17	0	0	11,573.17	11,573.17
RM110820	3000	301	9,700	3,977.65	2,177.65	1	2,177.65	2,177.65
RM120325	3000	313	148,134	104,004.88	0	0	104,004.88	104,004.88
RM110900	3000	310	15,000	13,500	?	0	13,500	13,500

154

Below is the overall layout of the Calculation view

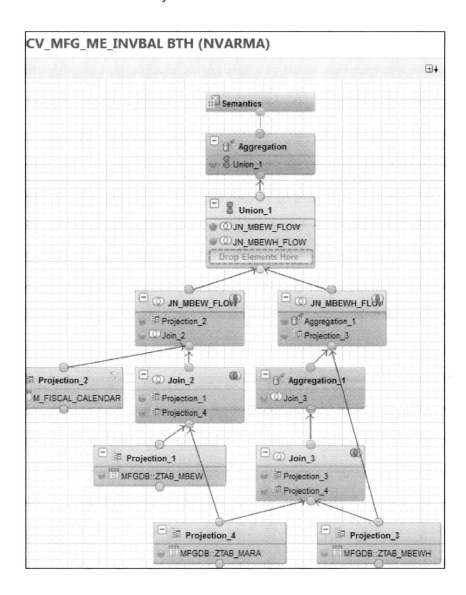

Detailed steps to implement this calculation view:

Projection on ZTAB_MBEWH Table

Create a calculated column to concatenate the Year (LFGJA) and Month (LFMON) as a single field.

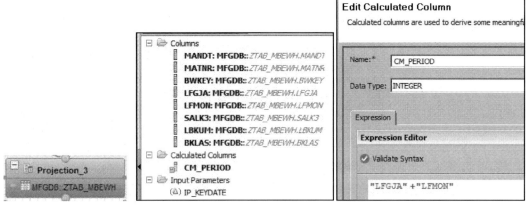

Create the following input parameter: For the Key Date used to derive the month end balances

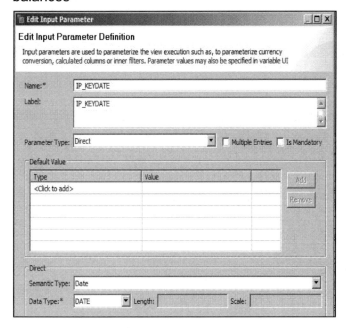

Projection on MARA table: This is mainly to derive the Material Type (MTART)

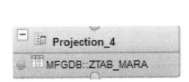
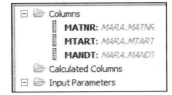

Join on both projection of MBEWH and MARA: Join type: Left outer

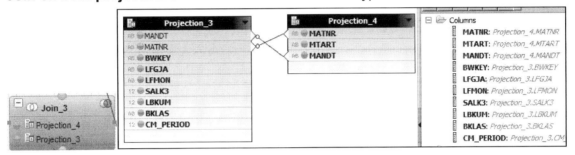

Aggregation_1: To derive the stock value for the latest period for each material from MBEWH

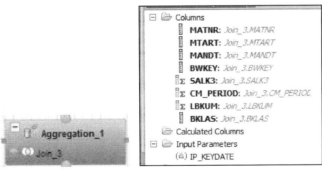

Set the following aggregation properties to the measures:

SALK3: Sum
CM_PERIOD: Max
LBKUM: Sum

Implement the following join to derive the Stock values for the latest period for each of the materials (Join type: Inner Join)

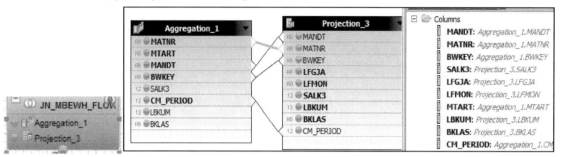

Projection on MBEW: Create a calculated column which stores the Key Date given as Input

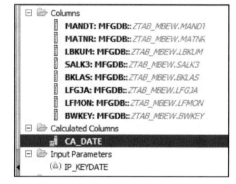

Create the calculated column as shown below

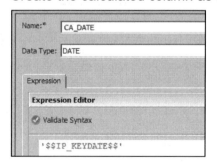

SAP® HANA Modeling Practical World | HANA Modeling Practical Case studies

Join on MBEW and MARA: (Left outer join)

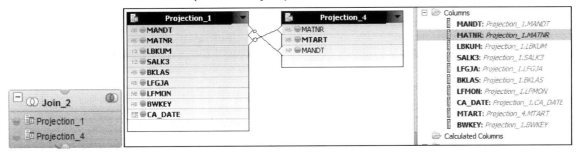

Projection on Time Dimension table:

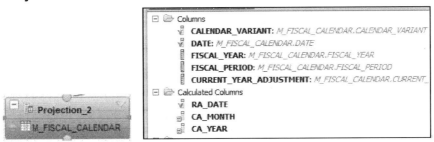

Implement following calculated columns

CA_MONTH and CA_YEAR are used to derive the Previous Month / Year for the Key Date.

Name	Type	Data Type & Length	Formula
RA_DATE	Attribute	DATE	$$IP_KEYDATE$$
CA_MONTH	Attribute	INTEGER	IF(int("FISCAL_PERIOD")>1, int("FISCAL_PERIOD") – 1, 12)
CA_YEAR	Attribute	INTEGER	IF(int("FISCAL_PERIOD")>1, int("FISCAL_YEAR" , int("FISCAL_YEAR") – 1)

Apply the following filter expression:

`("CALENDAR_VARIANT" = 'K4') and date("DATE") ="RA_DATE"`

159

Join MBEW flow with the time dimension:

This join is essential used to get all the required time dimension attributes for the key date.

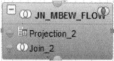

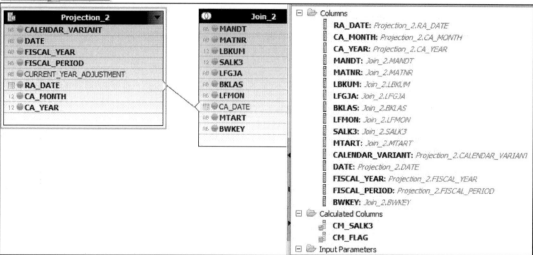

Implement Calculated Columns as per the below definitions:

Derive the material stock from MBEW

Name	Type	Data Type & Length	Formula
CM_SALK3	Measure	DECIMAL (15,2)	IF(int("LFGJA") < "CA_YEAR","SALK3",IF((int("LFGJA") ="CA_YEAR" AND int("LFMON") <="CA_MONTH"),"SALK3",0))
CM_FLAG	Attribute	INTEGER	IF(int("LFGJA") < "CA_YEAR",1,IF((int("LFGJA") ="CA_YEAR" AND int("LFMON") <="CA_MONTH"),1,0))

Union of both the data flows (MBEW and MBEWH)

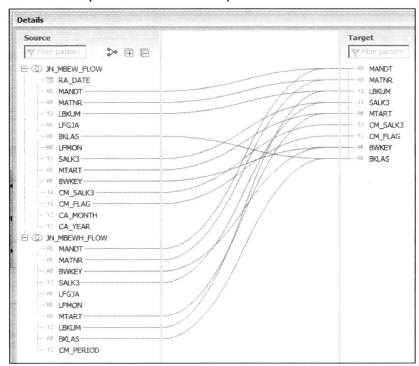
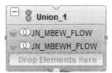

Note: CM_SALK3 and CM_FLAG fields are mapped only from JN_MBEW_FLOW. Remaining target columns are mapped from both the sources to the identical columns.

Final aggregation node:

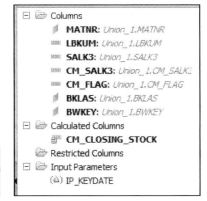
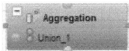

Set the Aggregation behavior of all the above measures to "Sum"

Create calculated column for the **Closing Stock (CM_CLOSING_STOCK)**. In this we are deriving the closing stock value either from the MBEWH or from MBEW, based on the period

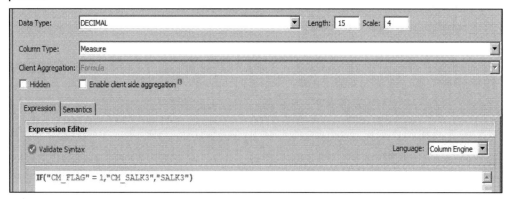

Activate the calculation view.

Validate results of the calculation view: The Closing stock values are shown as expected.

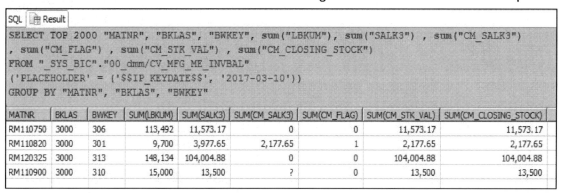

Concept check: We have used the following features to implement the solution:
- ✓ Union node – To combine the period end inventory values of the materials that has the entries in two different sources
- ✓ Calculated columns: To implement formulas based on certain conditions to derive the closing stock for each material
- ✓ Aggregation types: using Max, Sum depending on the scenario

5.4 Business Case: Calculating Cumulative Sales Revenues

Requirement Description: Cumulative measures are used to generate the running totals for various KPIs. These are needed in some of the reporting scenarios. In this scenario, we need to produce the Cumulative Sales Revenue for each of the Calendar Months in the given selection criteria.

Key Concepts:
- Table Types Definition
- Table Functions
- Consuming Table Functions in Graphical Calculation Views

Step #1: Create Table Type and Table Function with the following logic – This table function will return the set of Calendar Months which are supposed to be considered for Cumulative calculations of each of the Calendar Months.

Note: In SQL Script we can define table types or structures as global data types to reuse them across multiple functions or procedures. The extension to be used for defining the structure is **.hdbstructure.**

As part of this solution we need to build the following Table Type / Structure:

```
Table Type: 00_dmm:ZTT_CUMM_MONTHS.hdbstructure
table.schemaName = "NVARMA" ;
table.tableType = COLUMNSTORE;
table.columns = [
{name = "CALMONTH" ; sqlType = NVARCHAR ; length = 6;} ,
{name = "CUMM_MONTH" ; sqlType = NVARCHAR;  length = 6 ;}
];
```

		SAP® HANA Modeling		HANA Modeling Practical Case studies

Implement the following table function and use the above Table Type in the signature to represent the returning Table Variable.

Table Function: 00_dmm::TF_SALES_CUMM_MONTHS.hdbtablefunction

```
FUNCTION "NVARMA"."00_dmm::TF_SALES_CUMM_MONTHS" ( )
    RETURNS "NVARMA"."00_dmm::ZTT_CUMM_MONTHS"
    LANGUAGE SQLSCRIPT
    SQL SECURITY INVOKER AS
BEGIN
```

--For every CALMONTH Return the set of Cumulative CALMONTHs
```
RETURN SELECT DISTINCT A.CALMONTH , B.CALMONTH as "CUMM_MONTH"
        from "_SYS_BI"."M_TIME_DIMENSION" as A
    INNER JOIN "_SYS_BI"."M_TIME_DIMENSION" as B
        ON B.CALMONTH <= A.CALMONTH and B.YEAR = A.YEAR
        WHERE A.YEAR between '2010' and '2024' ;
END;
```

> **Concept check:** We have implemented the *self-join* in the above table function to get all previous months of each month. Self-join is the operation where both the tables involved in the join are same.

Testing the Table Function:

Note: Table Functions are like the virtual data models (information views). Hence, we can query them in the similar way as the Calculation Views.

```
select * from  "NVARMA"."00_dmm::TF_SALES_CUMM_MONTHS"() where CALMONTH = '201110'
```

	CALMONTH	CUMM_MONTH
1	201110	201110
2	201110	201101
3	201110	201102
4	201110	201103
5	201110	201104
6	201110	201105
7	201110	201106
8	201110	201107
9	201110	201108
10	201110	201109

Step #2: Build Calculation view with the following layout and properties, as per the following steps

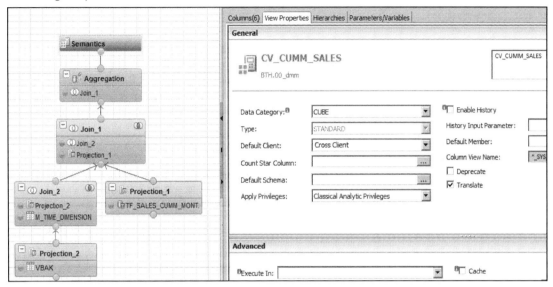

Projection on VBAK table

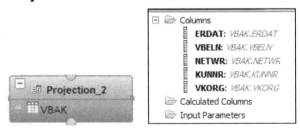

Join node with TIME dimension table: (Join type: Left Outer)

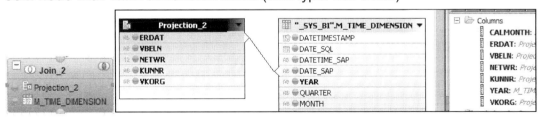

Note: Add YEAR and CALMONTH fields from M_TIME_DIMENSION to output

Projection node for Table Function to get Cumulative months

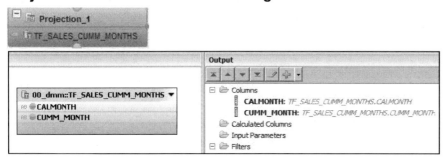

Join node to map the Sales Orders flow with the Table function for cumulative months (Join type: Inner join)

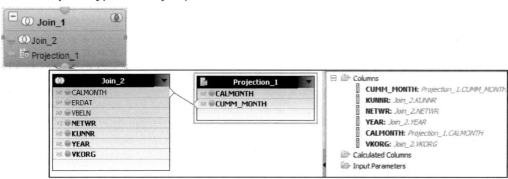

Concept check: We are consuming the Table function in a graphical calculation view here. We can also pass the values to the parameters of the table function using the "Input Parameter Mapping" feature

Final Aggregation node:

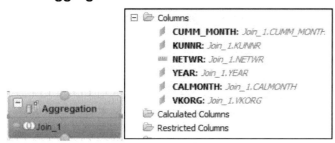

Data preview: Query the view results and observe the Cumulative values:

Case #1: Detailed results of Cumulative Months for each of the Calendar Month

```sql
SELECT
    "CALMONTH","YEAR","CUMM_MONTH",
    sum("NETWR") AS "NETWR"
FROM "_SYS_BIC"."00_dmm/CV_CUMM_SALES"
where ("CALMONTH" between '201301' and '201304')
    and VKORG = '1000'
GROUP BY "CUMM_MONTH", "YEAR", "CALMONTH", "VKORG"
Order by CALMONTH, CUMM_MONTH
```

	CALMONTH	YEAR	CUMM_MONTH	NETWR
1	201301	2013	201301	266,495.5
2	201302	2013	201301	266,495.5
3	201302	2013	201302	294,310
4	201303	2013	201301	266,495.5
5	201303	2013	201302	294,310
6	201303	2013	201303	286,824.9
7	201304	2013	201301	266,495.5
8	201304	2013	201302	294,310
9	201304	2013	201303	286,824.9
10	201304	2013	201304	277,161.6

Case #2: Cumulative Sales revenue for each of the Calendar Months in the given range

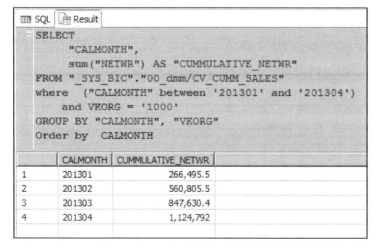

```sql
SELECT
    "CALMONTH",
    sum("NETWR") AS "CUMMULATIVE_NETWR"
FROM "_SYS_BIC"."00_dmm/CV_CUMM_SALES"
where ("CALMONTH" between '201301' and '201304')
    and VKORG = '1000'
GROUP BY "CALMONTH", "VKORG"
Order by CALMONTH
```

	CALMONTH	CUMMULATIVE_NETWR
1	201301	266,495.5
2	201302	560,805.5
3	201303	847,630.4
4	201304	1,124,792

6 Testing and Validation of HANA Models

HANA Modeling solutions are predominantly based on Graphical Calculation Views, which consists of a network of nodes of various types such as Joins, Unions, Projections and Aggregations. Quite commonly we will face challenges to validate the HANA view results, as the complexity of overall model increases. Hence it would be helpful to know the effective approaches to perform the validations and identify the issues in different scenarios.

Common data inconsistency issues in the calculation views:

- ➢ Duplicate records
- ➢ Improper aggregation of measures
- ➢ Incorrect results in formulas or counts
- ➢ Missing records in the result
- ➢ Filters not being applied correctly

6.1 Effective validation techniques for SAP HANA Calculation Views

This unit will provide some of the useful techniques to validate HANA calculation views. These techniques will be of good use to ensure proper unit testing & integration testing to avoid common data issues before delivering the models for user acceptance testing. These validation approaches will be equally helpful while implementing changes to the existing views as part of enhancements, bug fixes etc.

Below are the key tools and techniques to perform data validation of HANA views:

6.1.1 Data preview option:

Using the data preview option at the HANA view level and at the individual node level is the simplest option to validate the data during the development of HANA views. Leverage the various options such as raw data with filters, distinct value analysis, generating the SQL statement from the log etc. to perform different types of validations using the data preview option

- To view results of specific columns (attributes and measures) – Analysis tab
- To check distinct counts for attribute values – Distinct values tab
- To view the records based on certain filters – Raw Data tab
- Generated SQL statement – Show Log button

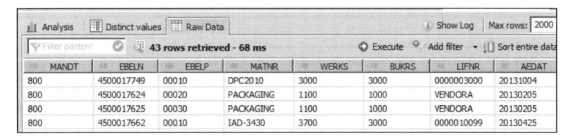

6.1.2 Validate HANA Views using Custom SQL queries:

We can write and execute custom SQL queries in HANA studio SQL editor, and compare the results of HANA view to ensure that the results are matching. Here we can leverage the various types of SQL statements to perform complex data validations - for example to compare the data between the HANA view and the base tables

Each of the nodes in a HANA calculation view will corresponding to an operation in SQL such as Join, Union etc. We can validate the results of any node by comparing with the results of an equivalent SQL statement to check if there is any deviation in the results.

How to verify if there are any duplicate records produced by HANA view?

One of the most frequently faced issues in the calculation views is the generation of duplicate records, which will impact the model in many ways such as multiplication of measures, slow performance due to the data volumes etc.

Let us understand the behavior of different SQL statements while checking the COUNT:

The query on the following view has fetched total of 176 records as shown below.

SAP® HANA Modeling Practical World	Testing and Validation of HANA Models

```
SQL | Result
SELECT * from "_SYS_BIC"."00_dmm/CV_LATEST_CUSTOMER_ORDER"
```

	MANDT	KUNNR	ERDAT	VKORG	KDGRP	NETWR
1	800	0000001000	20150408	3000		0
2	800	0000003250	20140205	3000		56,000
3	800	0000003286	20141107	3000		1,500
4	800	0000003287	20141107	3000		2,500
5	800	0000003289	20140418	3000		11,000
6	800	0000003410	20140418	3000		40,000
7	800	0000003411	20140418	3000		11,000
8	800	0000003413	20141107	3000		500

```
Statement 'SELECT * from "_SYS_BIC"."00_dmm/CV_LATEST_CUSTOMER_ORDER"'
successfully executed in 20 ms 529 µs  (server processing time: 19 ms 721 µs)
Fetched 176 row(s) in 3 ms 604 µs (server processing time: 1 ms 428 µs)
```

However if we execute the COUNT(*) on this view, we are seeing a different result, which is incorrect. The reason for this discrepancy is, because the below query performs the count of records before the final aggregation.

```
SELECT count(*) from "_SYS_BIC"."00_dmm/CV_LATEST_CUSTOMER_ORDER"
```

	COUNT(*)
1	183

To get the correct count of records on a Calculation View always use the query as shown below.

SELECT Count(*) FROM

(Select * from <Calculation view> [Filter conditions]);

```
SQL | Result
SELECT Count (*) from
  (SELECT * from "_SYS_BIC"."00_dmm/CV_LATEST_CUSTOMER_ORDER")
```

	COUNT(*)
1	176

170

| SAP® HANA Modeling | Testing and Validation of HA |
| Practical World | |

To identify the duplicate records generated in a calculation view we can use the following query:

For example if the records of the view should be identified uniquely by KUNNR – We can use the below query to identify if there any specific customer (KUNNR) records with duplicates.

```
Select kunnr from (
Select kunnr, count(*) from
"_SYS_BIC"."00_dmm/CV_LATEST_CUSTOMER_ORDER"
Group by kunnr
Having count(*) > 1)
```

How to compare two different version of a HANA view to check if the results are matching?

Sometimes we will create multiple version of a calculation view to identify the best approach from performance point of view. However we need to ensure that these different versions will produce the same results. We can compare the results of multiple queries using the MINUS operator in SQL, which returns all the non-matching records (if there are any).

```
SELECT <Columns> from <View_A>
MINUS
SELECT <Columns> from <View_B> ;
```

This query should not fetch any rows, if both the views are producing the same results.

6.1.3 Calculation View debugging for node level validation of data:

The recent versions of HANA modeling toolset contain the calculation view debugging feature which can be used to perform node by node analysis of calculation views. Even though we can use the Data Preview option in each of the nodes in a calculation view, the calculation view debugging provides more intuitve and rich functionality to validate the results.

Below are some of the key benefits of this tool and especially how it helps us in comparison to the node level data preview functionality.

1. Flexibility to customize the generated SQL statement with required filters to perform debugging on selective records across the nodes in the data flow. This will really help us in tracing the results for a particular selection of records at each node level and identify the issues easily.

- For example, we need to validate the results of a calculation for a specific Material number

Explore the various steps to perform Calculation View Debugging:

- Start the debug session: Use the options shown below to start the calculation view debugging session.

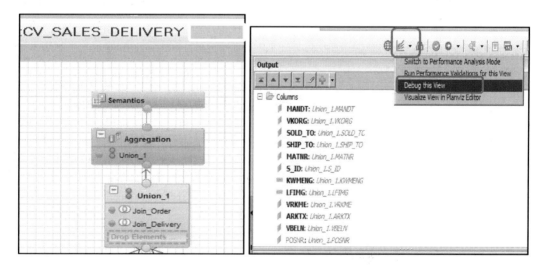

It will display the "Generated query"

```
SELECT "MANDT", "VKORG", "SOLD_TO", "SHIP_TO",
"MATNR", "S_ID", SUM("KWMENG"), SUM("LFIMG"), "VRKME",
    "ARKTX", "VBELN"
FROM "_SYS_BIC"."TRAINING_DEMO/CV_SALES_DELIVERY"
GROUP BY "MANDT", "VKORG",
    "SOLD_TO", "SHIP_TO", "MATNR", "S_ID", "VRKME",
    "ARKTX", "VBELN"
```

- Make necessary changes (For example: adding WHERE Clause as shown below) in the SQL query and run the debugger by choosing the Execute option

```
SELECT "MANDT", "VKORG", "SOLD_TO", "SHIP_TO",
"MATNR", "S_ID", SUM("KWMENG"), SUM("LFIMG"), "VRKME",
    "ARKTX", "VBELN"
FROM "_SYS_BIC"."TRAINING_DEMO/CV_SALES_DELIVERY"
where MATNR = 'M-19'
GROUP BY "MANDT", "VKORG",
    "SOLD_TO", "SHIP_TO", "MATNR", "S_ID", "VRKME",
    "ARKTX", "VBELN"
```

- It will open the Debugging session for this Calculation view – Choose the required node and run the query (In this case we have selected the node PR_VBAP)

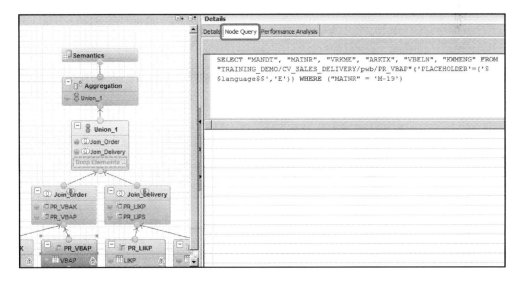

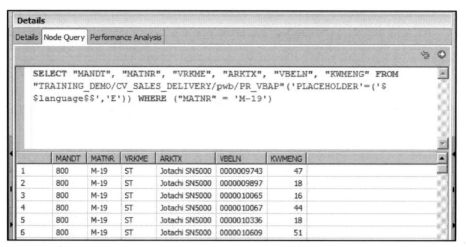

This will help us to perform node level debugging for specific selection of records in a very effective manner.

2. Implement the changes on the fly and continue with debugging – Once we start with the debugging of calculation view, if we find any issue that needs a change in the calculation view design, we can perform this change parallelly without closing the debugger session. After the changes are completed and the view is activated, we can validate the results instantly in the debugger session. This will certainly help in improving productivity.

3. Drill down to the inner calculation views in a stacked model: While debugging the main calculation view, we can also navigate to the inner calculation views and debug the nodes of these sub views. This will allow us to perform detailed analysis of the model within a single debug session.

Click on the drill down for debugging sub views from main calculation view debugging session

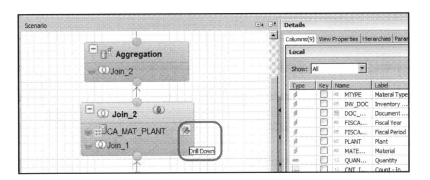

4. Verify the performance statistics of the source tables: Whenever the calculation view node has a Table as data source, we will be able to verify the key performance statistics (number of records, partitioning properties etc.) of the table instantly in the debug session.

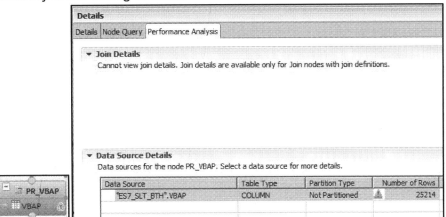

6.2 Preparing Test Plans for HANA Models

Testing is an essential phase in any of the IT projects. Hence it is certainly desirable to have proper planning along with appropriate tools and techniques to perform the testing successfully and minimize the defects and rework.

6.2.1 Validation criteria for HANA views

Prepare a comprehensive data validation and test plans for your HANA views. Ensure that your test cases will include the validation of the attributes and measures along with all the key functionalities such as:

- Filters, Calculations, Aggregations, Counters, Currency and unit conversions
- Input selections: Variables and Input parameters
- Performance of HANA views

6.2.2 Sample test plan for a Calculation View:

Below is a sample test plan to validate the HANA views to ensure that the results are meeting the overall requirements of the KPIs.

Test Step	Test category	Step Name	Step Description	Expected Result	Actual Result
1	Data Reconciliation	Validate data (Facts and dimensions)	Perform the data preview to check if the output of the view is matching – Including the Count of records	The dimensions and measures should match with the source tables	Values are shown as expected in the calculation view
3	Filters and selections	Check if all the user inputs and filter conditions are working	Try to query the view with the different set of input values and validate the output	Output records should be shown correctly as per the filters	Output records are shown correctly as per the filters
4	Calculations and aggregation behavior	Validate aggregated calculations	Validate the calculation at a summarized level and ensure that the calculation is happening at the right level	The manual calculation should match with the calculated measure	Manual calculations are matching with the calculated measure

7 Smart Tools and Techniques for Productivity

There are several tools and options available in the HANA studio, which helps us in troubleshooting the issues, maintaining the views in a simplified manner and increase the productivity. Let us understand how to leverage these tools and features while building and maintaining HANA views.

7.1 Tools and options to simplify the HANA modeling process

Implementing complex calculation views involves connecting various nodes of different type and setting up the properties for each of the nodes and respective columns as well. In this process it is very much essential for us to utilize the available tools and options to simplify the process of developing and maintaining the models.

Listed below are some of these tools and their utility in HANA modeling process:

7.1.1 Trace the Origin of Columns (Show Lineage):

In some scenarios we need to trace the origin of a specific attribute or measure in HANA views. We can achieve this using the "Show Lineage" option in the "Semantics" node.

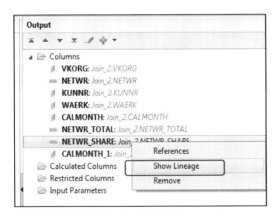
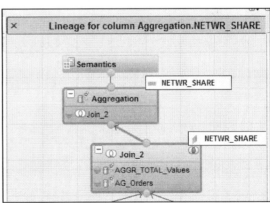

7.1.2 Find the column usage (References):

Whenever you need to change or remove a specific column in the HANA calculation view, it is advisable to verify the usage and impact of that column, to avoid breaking the related

| SAP® HANA Modeling Practical World | Smart Tools and Techniques for Productivity |

joins, calculations etc. which are dependent on that column. We can achieve this using the "References" option for a specific column.

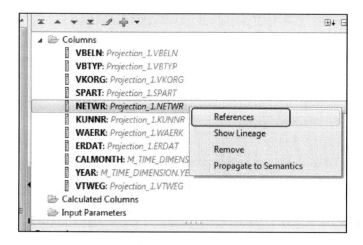

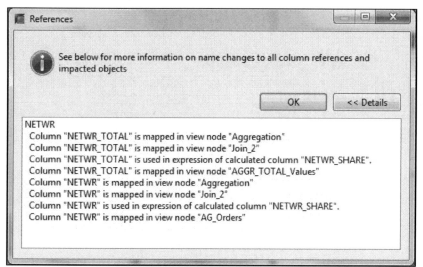

In the above details, we will be able to identify the various nodes, formulas and other modeling elements which are based on this specific column.

7.1.3 Replacing nodes and data sources (In graphical calculation views)

In different scenarios we need to replace the existing data source or node in the overall calculation view. We can use the following option to replace the nodes (projection, join..) with a different node OR replace the data sources (views or tables) with a different view or table within a modeled view.

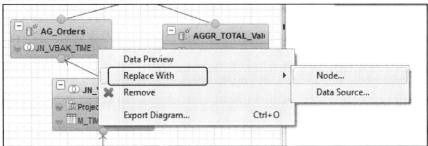

Whenever we need to remove an unwanted node in the calculation view, we can use the "Replace Node" option and choose the new node in the lower level model.

7.1.4 Inserting nodes in the existing data flow (In calculation views)

Quite commonly we need to add new nodes within the data flow of a calculation view. For example, inserting new Join between the two nodes to derive new set of columns, or adding extra projection node for filtering data between two nodes.
To add a new node between two existing nodes:
- Choose the respect node template (Example: Join)
- Drag and drop it on the "Arrow Line", which is connecting the desired pair of nodes. (As shown below)

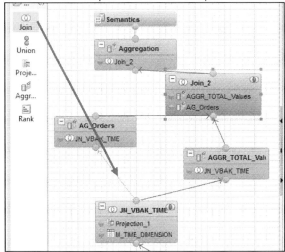

179

7.1.5 Generate Select SQL

Using this option, we can get the generated SELECT statement for any of the HANA views, which can be customized and executed from the SQL editor

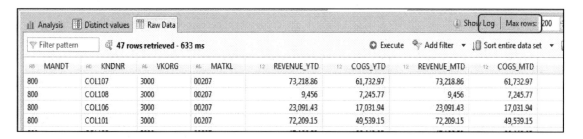

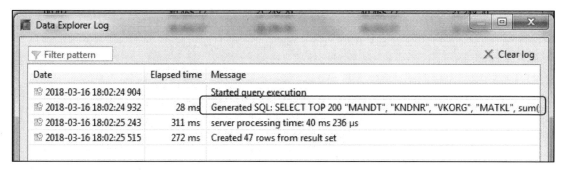

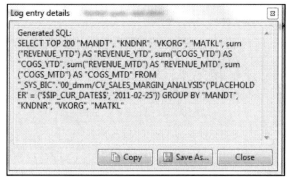

Open the SQL Editor and paste this query to modify and execute it further.

7.1.6 Mass Copy and Refactoring of Information views:

Refactoring: Using this option we can move the views across the packages, which automatically adjusts the inner views to reflect the new package. Refactoring also allows us to rename the view.

Mass Copy: Using this option we can copy a set of information views from one package to another package. This is very useful when we need to copy all our models from temporary package to the main package.

7.1.7 Where-used list:

To identify the list of objects which are using a specific HANA development artifact like Calculation view, Table function etc. we can use this Where Used List option. This will help us to assess the impact of any changes

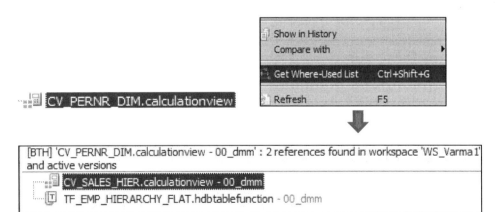

7.2 Version Management of HANA Development Objects

Versioning will be an essential feature of the development objects, since it allows us to track the various changes related to the object and switch the object to specific version whenever needed.

How to view the versions of HANA development objects
From the popup menu of the calculation view: Choose "Show in History". This will show all the list of versions which are generated during the previous activations.

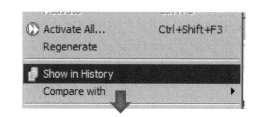

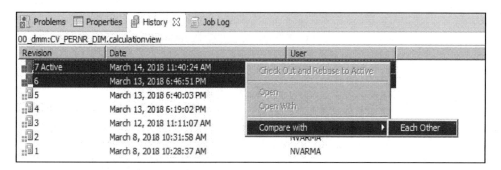

How to compare two different version of a repository object

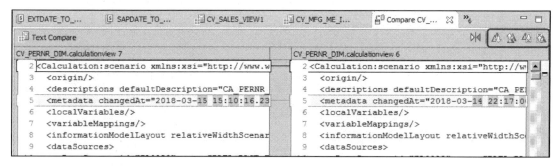

Switching the repository object to specific version

00_dmm:CV_PERNR_DIM.calculationview		
Revision	Date	User
7 Active [Base]	March 14, 2018 11:40:24 AM	NVARMA
6	March 13, 2018 6:46:51 PM	Check Out and Rebase to Active
5	March 13, 2018 6:40:03 PM	
4	March 13, 2018 6:19:02 PM	Open

Using the "Check out and Rebase to Active" option we can switch the object to any of the previous active versions

7.3 Tips for leveraging Built-in Tables in HANA

There are numerous standard tables in SAP HANA to store the metadata such as User Profiles, Calculation view properties, Query statistics etc. Understanding these tables and views will help us in exploring the necessary details in various scenarios. Following are the few examples on how to query the standard tables in troubleshooting different issues.

Identify the usage of tables in HANA

How to identify the list of HANA views in which a specific database table has been used? Execute a query on SYS.OBJECT_DEPENDENCIES Table with appropriate selection.

```sql
SELECT DISTINCT
        "BASE_SCHEMA_NAME",
        "BASE_OBJECT_NAME",
        "DEPENDENT_SCHEMA_NAME",
        "DEPENDENT_OBJECT_NAME"
FROM
        "SYS"."OBJECT_DEPENDENCIES"
WHERE
        "DEPENDENT_OBJECT_NAME" LIKE '%'
        AND "BASE_OBJECT_NAME" LIKE '%EKPO%'
        AND "BASE_OBJECT_TYPE" = 'TABLE'
        AND "DEPENDENT_OBJECT_NAME" LIKE '%00_dmm%'
```

	BASE_SCHEMA_NAME	BASE_OBJECT_NAME	DEPENDENT_SCHEMA_NAME	DEPENDENT_OBJECT_NAME
1	ES7_SLT_BTH	EKPO	PUBLIC	00_dmm::CV_OPEN_PO
2	ES7_SLT_BTH	EKPO	_SYS_BIC	00_dmm/CV_OPEN_PO
3	ES7_SLT_BTH	EKPO	_SYS_BIC	00_dmm/CV_OPEN_PO/AEDAT/hier/AEDAT
4	ES7_SLT_BTH	EKPO	_SYS_BIC	00_dmm/CV_OPEN_PO/BUKRS/hier/BUKRS

To verify the modified objects by a user or during a specific time

Refer to ACTIVE_OBJECT table in _SYS_REPO schema.

	SQL	Result

```
select * from _SYS_REPO.active_object where OBJECT_NAME = 'CV_PERNR_DIM'
```

	PACKAGE_ID	OBJECT_NAME	OBJECT_SUFFIX	VERSION_ID	ACTIVATED_AT	ACTIVATED_BY
1	00_dmm	CV_PERNR_DIM	calculationview	7	Mar 15, 2018 4:40:24.706 AM	NVARMA

Useful tables related to the Security – Roles and Privileges

- List of privileges assigned to a specific user: SYS.EFFECTIVE_PRIVILEGES Table
- List of roles granted to specific user: SYS.GRANTED_ROLES Table

SQL	Result

```
Select * from SYS.EFFECTIVE_PRIVILEGES
where USER_NAME = 'NVARMA' and OBJECT_TYPE = 'ANALYTICALPRIVILEGE'
```

USER_NAME	GRAN...	GRANTEE	GRANTEE_TYPE	GRANTOR_SCH...	GRANTOR	GRANTOR_TYPE	OBJECT_TYPE	SCHE...	OBJECT_NAME
NVARMA	?	NVARMA	USER	?	_SYS_REPO	USER	ANALYTICALPRIVILEGE	?	sap.hana.democontent.epm.models/AP_
NVARMA	?	MODELING	ROLE	?	_SYS_REPO	USER	ANALYTICALPRIVILEGE	?	_SYS_BI_CP_ALL
NVARMA	?	NVARMA	USER	?	MODELING	ROLE	ANALYTICALPRIVILEGE	?	_SYS_BI_CP_ALL
NVARMA	?	CONTE...	ROLE	?	_SYS_REPO	USER	ANALYTICALPRIVILEGE	?	_SYS_BI_CP_ALL

Query Performance Statistics related tables

You would like to know which HANA views are being consumed by which users along with some statistics about the performance of these views over a period of time. We may have to look at stats tables in HANA and see if there is any Views already created on top of the stats tables to get info like this.

View: M_SQL_PLAN_CACHE

```
select USER_NAME, STATEMENT_STRING, TOTAL_EXECUTION_TIME,
TOTAL_EXECUTION_MEMORY_SIZE, TOTAL_RESULT_RECORD_COUNT,
LAST_EXECUTION_TIMESTAMP
from M_SQL_PLAN_CACHE where STATEMENT_STRING like '%FROM
"_SYS_BIC"."00_dmm%'
```

View: M_EXPENSIVE_STATEMENTS

Example: We need to know the list of expensive statements produced by the views from specific package and by particular user.

```
select * from SYS.M_EXPENSIVE_STATEMENTS
where DB_USER = 'NVARMA' and STATEMENT_STRING like   '%FROM
"_SYS_BIC"."00_dmm%'
```

8 Performance Tuning Techniques for HANA models

One of the key reasons for the wide adoption of SAP HANA platform is its capability of delivering high performance while querying data. In general, the users will expect faster response times while running the reports and performing drill down operations. Hence it is very essential to analyze the performance of HANA models to ensure the optimal run time, memory and CPU utilization. Let us look at the standard tools and techniques to analyze the HANA model performance in various scenarios.

Key factors that will generally influence the performance of various queries in HANA database:

1) Volume of records processed during the operations such as aggregation or join

2) Number of attributes and measures in the query – remember the column engine performs best when the number of columns is kept to minimal

3) Different execution engines which are to be involved during the query execution and the amount of data to be transferred between them - Whenever the query processing needs to switch between different engines, all the intermediate results need to be temporarily materialized, which can cause memory and performance issues.

4) Specific type of formulas, expressions used in the HANA models that might consume high amount of memory

5) Different physical locations (nodes and partitions) to be accessed and the amount of data to be transferred between them

8.1 Performance analysis tools in HANA

SAP HANA has various built-in tools that can be utilized to measure the performance of the queries. As per the specific scenario, we can use the following tools to analyze the performance.

- Plan Visualizer (PlanViz) tool
- Explain Plan Tool
- SQL Trace Tool
- Expensive Statement Trace

8.2 Using Plan Visualizer Tool for Query Performance Analysis

This is the most useful tool to analyze the performance of overall HANA model to understand the key statistics of query execution such as.

- Overall run time & Which are the dominant operations taking maximum run time
- Node level statistics
- Filters applied on various tables
- Memory allocation
- Parallelization of operations
- Usage of various engines at different nodes (Calculation engine, OLAP engine.)

Since Plan Visualizer provides the most comprehensive performance statistics of a query execution in HANA, we need to understand the various details that can be analyzed and the navigation paths to achieve this.

Options to run a query under Plan Visualizer:

We can use the following methods to run a SELECT query through Plan Visualizer:

- In SQL editor use the Visualize Plan option from the menu:

Right click on the SQL query and choose Visualize Plan → Execute

```
SELECT "VKORG", "SPART", "KUNNR", "WAERK", "CALMONTH", "VTWEG", "YEAR",
sum("NETWR") AS "NETWR", sum("NETWR_TOTAL") AS "NETWR_TOTAL", sum("NETWR_SHARE") AS "NETWR_SHARE"
  FROM "_SYS_BIC"."00_dmm/CV_SALES_DYNJOIN"
  GROUP BY "VKORG", "SPART", "KUNNR", "WAERK", "CALMONTH", "VTWEG", "YEAR";
```

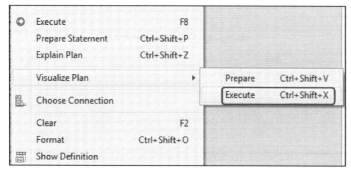

This will switch to PlanViz perspective.

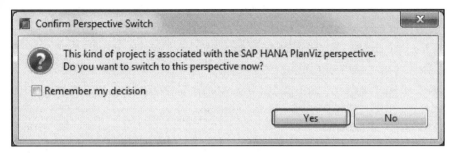

After this the system will run the query under the plan visualizer tool, which generates the detailed plan which is shown under Planviz perspective and also available as a file (.plv) which can be accessed offline.

Follow the below navigation paths to leverage the plan visualization to analyze the performance of query in multiple ways.

Identify operators with highest processing time:

Whenever we see an opportunity to optimize the performance of HANA views, the first thing that we would be curious to know is:

- Which are the most time-consuming operations in the overall query?

In the Overview tab of Plan Visualization results, we will find the dominant operators, which shows top 3 operations of the overall query based on the processing time. This will allow us to directly navigate to those specific operations and identify the possible reasons. Further, we can switch to the details such as "Operator list" to identify the performance aspects of various operations during the query execution

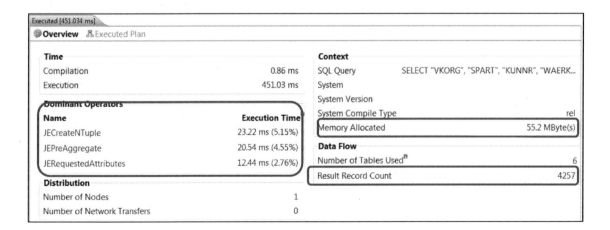

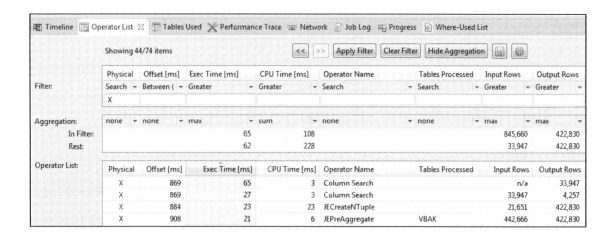

Check table access and filter push down operations:

To achieve optimal performance for a query, one of the essential criteria is to ensure that the dataset is minimized at the very beginning, while fetching the records from the source tables (particularly the tables with larger volumes). Through PlanViz Table access and Operator List tabs we can verify the list of tables along with the number of accesses. (This list also includes the temporary tables generated during the execution).

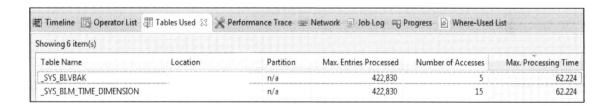

In the Operator List, if we search for "Basic Predicate" we will find the filter operations on the tables (as shown below). Whenever we see the filter conductions at the Basic Predicate level on the database table, that means it is performing the filter pushdown.

SAP® HANA Modeling Practical World | Performance Tuning Techniques for HANA models

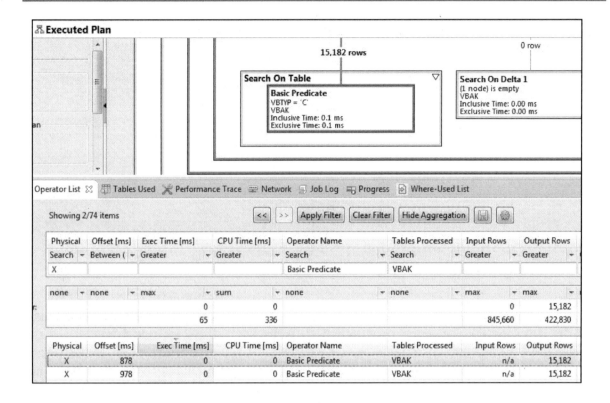

View Timelines to identify the bottleneck nodes:

Using the Timeline view, we can visually identify the operations which are acting as bottleneck to the performance, operations which are running in parallel and drill down to the specific operation for further analysis.

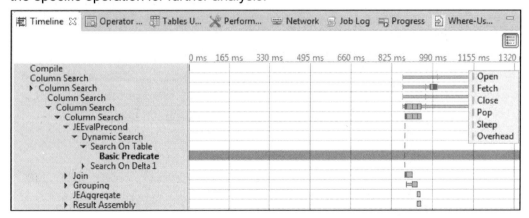

| SAP® HANA Modeling Practical World | Performance Tuning Techniques for HANA models |

8.2.1 Understand the individual operators in the Visualization Plan:

We will get the following details at the node level in the generated plan.

Name: JEAggregate
ID: X2_plan4630234_tlihanabth_30003_pop14
Summary: SUM (NETWR)
Schema:
Execution Time (Inclusive): 59.892 ms
Execution Time (Exclusive): 10.607 ms
Execution Start Time: 928.896 ms
Execution End Time: 939.503 ms
CPU Time (User): 10.668 ms
Table/column Processed 001: VBAK.NETWR

Press 'F2' or hover the cursor over th

JEAggregate
SUM (NETWR)
VBAK.NETWR
Inclusive Time: 59.9 ms
Exclusive Time: 10.6 ms

Node name: Determines the type of operation and the processing engine

Execution Time:

Inclusive time: Processing time of all the operations related to this node

Exclusive time: Processing time specific to this operations. This is more relevant when we are looking for the long running operations

Tables / Columns Processed

8.3 Explain Plan Functionality

When we execute a SQL query in HANA the optimizer prepares an execution plan, which is in turn used to run the query. We can use the Explain Plan tool to understand the sequence of operations, engines involved, filters etc.

Using the Explain plan tool, we can analyze the execution plan which is created and optimized by the SQL optimizer. These plans are created based on runtime information about the query and data (e.g. number of records, data distribution etc.) as well as table statistics (if available). During the actual execution of query, additional optimizations are applied by the execution engines (e.g. column pruning in the calculation engine, join ordering in the join engine, removal of superfluous joins, etc.)

That means, using the explain plan we cannot analyze the actual query execution runtime. However it will provide us various insights in the execution plan to understand the potential areas of improvement.

SAP® HANA Modeling Practical World — Performance Tuning Techniques for HANA models

```sql
SELECT "VKORG", "SPART", "KUNNR", "WAERK", "CALMONTH", "VTWEG", "YEAR",
  sum("NETWR") AS "NETWR", sum("NETWR_TOTAL") AS "NETWR_TOTAL", sum("NETWR_SHARE") AS "NETWR_SHARE"
  FROM "_SYS_BIC"."00_dmm/CV_SALES_DYNJOIN"
  GROUP BY "VKORG", "SPART", "KUNNR", "WAERK", "CALMONTH", "VTWEG", "YEAR";
```

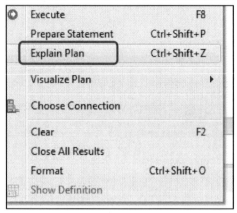

EXPLAIN PLAN FOR
SELECT "VKORG", "SPART", "KUNNR", "WAERK", "CALMONTH", "VTWEG", "YEAR",
sum("NETWR") AS "NETWR", sum("NETWR_TOTAL") AS "NETWR_TOTAL", sum("NETWR_SHARE") AS "NETWR_SHARE"
FROM "_SYS_BIC"."00_dmm/CV_SALES_DYNJOIN"
GROUP BY "VKORG", "SPART", "KUNNR", "WAERK", "CALMONTH", "VTWEG", "YEAR"

OPERATOR_NAME	OPERATOR_DETAILS	OPERATOR_PROPERT...	EXECUTION_ENGINE	TABLE_NAME	TABLE_TYPE	TABLE_SIZE	OUTPUT_SIZE
COLUMN SEARCH	VKORG, SPART, KUNNR, WAE...	LATE MATERIALIZATI...	COLUMN	?	?	?	14,350.872900000002
AGGREGATION	GROUPING: VBAK.VKORG, VB...		COLUMN	?	?	?	14,350
JOIN	JOIN CONDITION: (INNER) V...		COLUMN	?	?	?	15,106.182000000003
COLUMN TABLE	[FACT] FILTER CONDITION: V...		COLUMN	VBAK	COLUMN ...	15,918	15,106.181999999999
COLUMN SEARCH	M_TIME_DIMENSION.DATE_S...	ENUM_BY: CS_JOIN	COLUMN	#_SYS_QO_...	?	?	14,350.872900000002
AGGREGATION	GROUPING: VBAK.VKORG, VB...		COLUMN	?	?	?	14,350
JOIN	JOIN CONDITION: (INNER) V...		COLUMN	?	?	?	15,106.182
COLUMN TABLE	FILTER CONDITION: VBAK.VB...		COLUMN	VBAK	COLUMN ...	15,918	15,106.181999999999
COLUMN TABLE			COLUMN	M_TIME_DI...	COLUMN ...	11,326	11,326
COLUMN TABLE	[FACT]		COLUMN	M_TIME_DI...	COLUMN ...	11,326	11,326

8.4 Tracing Tools for HANA Queries

8.4.1 Expensive Statement Trace

Scenario: As part of the regular system monitoring, we need to identiry those queries which took longer to run and consumed more resources. For this we can activate the Expensive statement trace. These queries can be analyzed further by using the other tools like Plan visualizer to identify the possible improvements in the overall data model.

Below are the key beneifts of leverage the Expensive Statement Trace:
- Can be easily configured and allows us to focus on only those statements which are causing performance issues
- Provides information about runtimes of single statement executions
- Captures the parameter values for parameterized statements

How to Configure and Analyze:

We can activate the Expensive Statement Trace using the following option:

System Monitor → Trace Configuration → Expensive statement trace (Activate)

To review the expensive statement:

Administrator Perspective → HANA Instance → Performance → Expensive statement trace

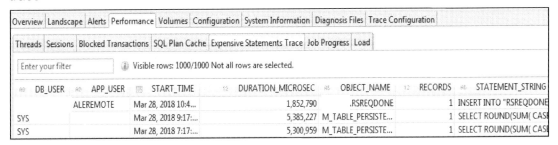

8.4.2 Using SQL Trace

We can activate the SQL trace in certain cases whete the queries sent from the front end tools need to be analyzed from performance point of view. For example, if the users are experiencinig

| SAP® HANA Modeling Practical World | Performance Tuning Techniques for HANA models |

Open the Administrator Perspective (System Monitor) of the respective HANA instance. In that situation, we can activate the SQL trace, request the user to run the report and stop the SQL trace to analyze the performance of the queries which are sent to HANA database.

Steps to utilize SQL Trace:

1) Activate SQL trace Administrator Perspective → HANA Instance → Trace configuration → SQL Trace

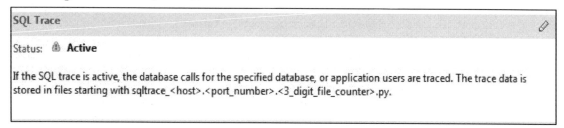

As a best practice, enter the User for whom the trace need to be run and the Table / Views etc.

This will ensure that the system will not generate the trace for wider scope of queries.

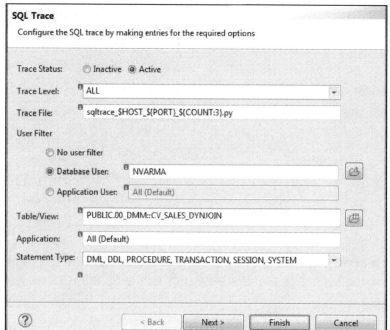

2) Execute the SQL statements:

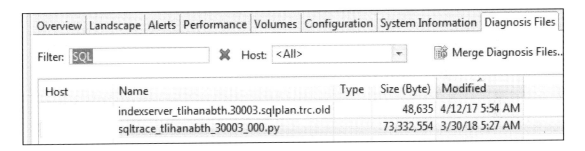

3) Verify the trace file, which shows the SQL statements which are executed by the user that are accessing the given table / views.

8.4.3 Plan Visualizer Example: Calculation view with Union Pruning

We have created the following calculation view with the Union Node pruning functionality. Let us analyze the execution plan and understand the benefits of Union Node pruning.

Run Plan visualizer on the below query:
```
select * from "_SYS_BIC"."00_dmm/CV_REGION_SALES" where BUKRS_VF = '2000';
```
Verify the results of Overview tab: Notice that the result record count is 3.

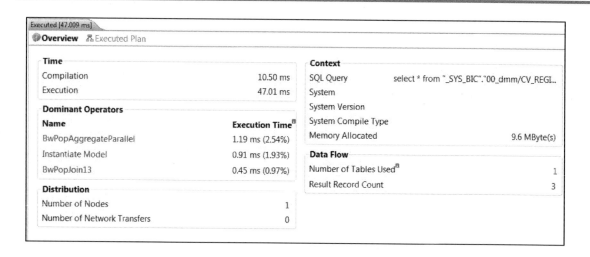

Verify the **Execution Plan** tab: We can observe the generated calculation model has three steps Initiate Model, Optimize Model and Execute Model.

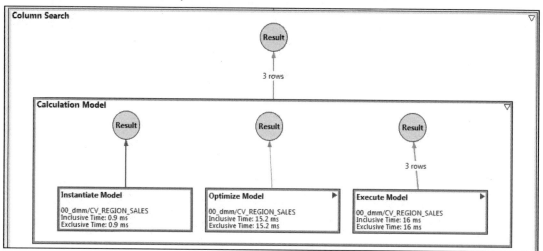

These steps will perform the union pruning operation by identifying the respective data sources of union nodes to be processed based on the entries maintained in the configuration table. In this case the filter condition on Company code (BUKRS_VF = 2000) will ensure that only the data source relevant for this company code is queried.

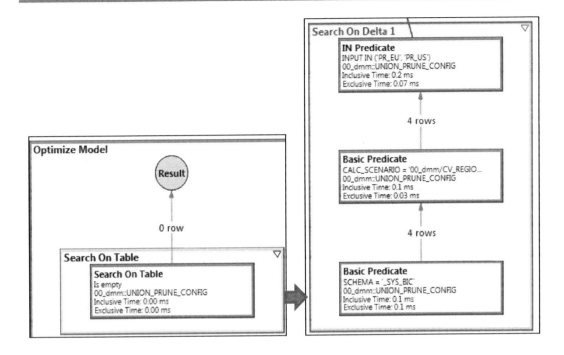

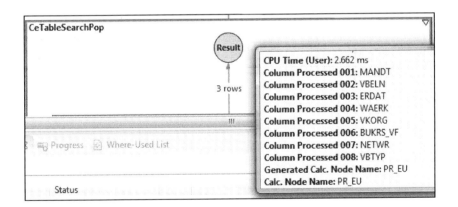

We can observe that the query has processed the union data source node PR_EU only since the company code belongs to EU region as maintained in the configuration table.

8.5 Calculation View – Performance Optimization Techniques

Try to explore some of the potential techniques to fine-tune the HANA view performance:

1) Filter on all appropriate data sources

2) Join optimization methods

3) Union Pruning or Constant column approach

4) Avoiding expensive aggregations

5) Formula level optimizations

6) Table Partitioning technique

7) View properties to optimize the processing

   - SQL Engine vs Column engine
   - Database Optimizer Hints

9 Transporting HANA Models

We need to have proper mechanism to transport the content from one HANA instance to another (Dev to QA to Production). In this unit, let us understand the key elements used to manage the HANA modeling artifacts along with the different methods of transporting HANA models.

9.1 Overview of Transport Mechanism for HANA data models

9.1.1 Transport Mechanisms for various use cases of HANA

Depending on the Enterprise application landscape and the HANA use case, we have various methods to transport the HANA development artifacts. Below table will provide the essential details to understand these transport methods and adopt the appropriate method as per the specific project needs.

HANA Use Case	Development Objects	Transport option
Native SAP HANA content	<ul><li>HANA Information views</li><li>Database objects</li><li>XS Development artifacts</li><li>Security objects</li></ul>	SAP HANA Application Lifecycle Management ✓ SAP HANA standalone transport management ✓ No need for ABAP footprint ✓ Lightweight and easy-to-use transport tool
Native SAP HANA content or as part of a solution (BW HANA Mixed, Suite on HANA, …)	<ul><li>HANA Information views</li><li>BW info providers</li><li>Security objects of both BW and HANA</li></ul>	Enhanced CTS (CTS+) ✓ Transported as any other non-ABAP content ✓ Integrated in existing CTS transport landscape ✓ Integrated in SAP process tools (Change Request Management, QGM)
SAP HANA content exclusively used by ABAP (ABAP for SAP HANA	<ul><li>HANA Information views</li><li>ABAP CDS Views</li></ul>	SAP HANA Transport Container ✓ Transported with standard ABAP transports ✓ Integrated in existing CTS transport landscape ✓ Integrated in SAP process tools (Change Request Management, QGM)

| SAP® HANA Modeling Practical World | Transporting HANA Models |

9.1.2 Naming standards for packages and modeling content

Define a package hierarchy using a specific naming strategy and ensure to create the HANA views under the appropriate packages. In addition, also maintain the ad-hoc packages for performing the changes to any views before they are moved to the main packages. This will help us to reduce the risk of impacting the existing models.

- ✓ Define and follow the appropriate naming conventions for information views and other development artifacts.
- ✓ Each developer can create and test the models in his/her own developer package. Once tested, the developer can re-create the models (by using Copy or Refactoring option) in appropriate package under project package structure.
- ✓ Developer need to ensure that the correct schema names and package names are referred in the models.

9.1.3 Importance of Schema Mappings

All the database objects must be defined under specific schema. Schemas acts as containers to group related database objects. It is generally recommended to have same schema names across all HANA systems (Dev, QA & Prod). If the source system schema names are different between HANA systems (Dev / QA / Prod), Schema Mapping functionality can be used in HANA Studio to map the physical HANA DB schema to Authoring schema. This will ensure that the development artifacts will work across the HANA system landscape. We can implement schema mappings in the Modeler perspective → Quick Launch tools.

9.1.4 Native HANA Application Lifecycle Management for Transports

SAP HANA Content (tables, views, procedures, functions etc.) can be transported using the of "Export and Import" - export from one HANA system and import into another. Packages and delivery units are the key entities used for transportation of content between HANA systems.

Every repository object in HANA must be created within a package. A package can contain number of objects of various types. Packages are mainly used to establish a namespace. In the repository, an object is uniquely identified by the combination of its package name, object name and object type. A package hierarchy can be created, establishing a parent- child type relationship between packages. To be able to transport the models, the respective packages must be assigned to Delivery Units.

A delivery unit is a logical grouping of packages. It defines a set of packages that are transported or shipped together. A delivery unit roughly corresponds to the concept of a software component, or in a customer's system, a project (or major unit of a project).

The export functionality allows us to export complete delivery units, including all packages and objects contained therein. In addition, dependencies can be defined between delivery units. This allows checking whether all references between objects from different delivery units are permitted through corresponding dependencies between delivery units. One of the key limitation of this approach is, we need to transport all the objects under a delivery unit, every time we made some changes to any of the objects. This will cause additional overhead in reviewing and monitoring the HANA transports.

9.2 Transporting HANA data models using Change Recording

Change Lists are introduced in SAP HANA to achieve more controlled mechanism of transporting the HANA modeling or development objects. Using the Change Lists we can transport only relevant objects across the landscape.

9.2.1 Enable Change Recording in HANA Application Lifecycle Managment

Background: SAP HANA Change Recording

When change recording enabled, you are prompted to assign your changes to a "Change List", while activating a repository object in development environment. Using change lists we can group all the objects that need to be transported together.

Step 1: Enable Change Recording in HANA system

This will be one-time configuration to be done by the administrator

Login as HANA Administrator and Launch the Life cycle management using Web IDE for HANA

https://<hana instance>:<port>/sap/hana/xs/lm/index.html

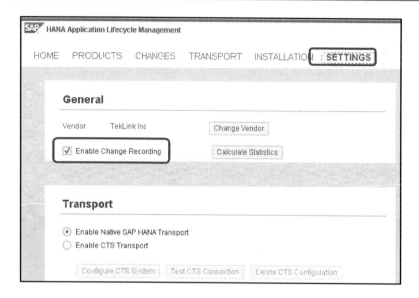

Step 2: **Assign required roles and privileges to HANA modelers**

Following System privileges need to be assigned to the HANA developers, to allow them to create new change lists and assign objects to the change lists and finally release change lists.

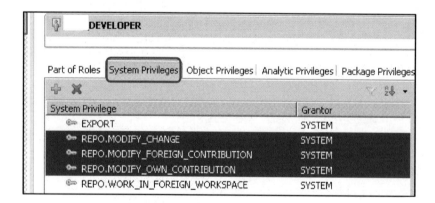

SAP® HANA Modeling Practical World — Transporting HANA Models

Step 3: Creating change lists

Login as HANA Developer

From Developer Perspective – Open the "Change Manager" view.

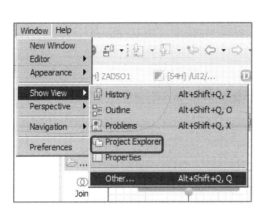
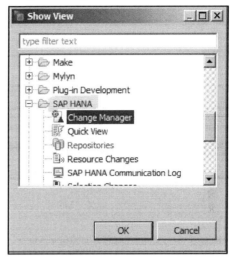

Change Manager view can be seen as shown below.

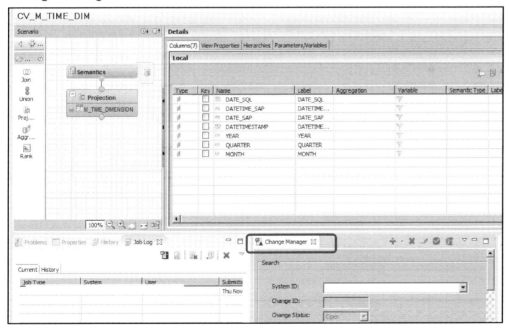

Maximize the Change manager view – Double click

203

SAP® HANA Modeling Practical World — Transporting HANA Models

Create new "Change List"

Enter relevant comment / description of the Change list (eg Defect #..)

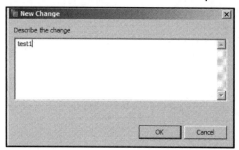

Choose the System ID to view the Change Lists under your user (Contributor)

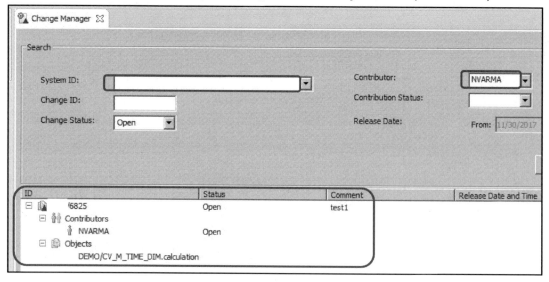

9.2.2 Release change lists for transport

"**Approve**" the objects of Contributor: Choose the contributor ID and click on the highlighted button.

Note: If there are more than one Contributor under the change list, each of them need to approve their contributions. Only then the owner of Change List will be able to release it.

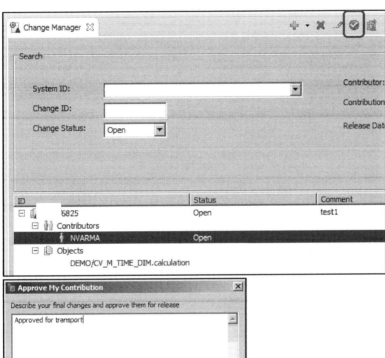

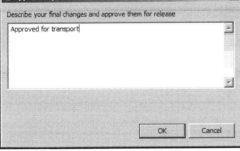

Enter comment and press OK.

"**Release**" Change List: Choose the Change List number and click on the highlighted button

SAP® HANA Modeling Practical World — Transporting HANA Models

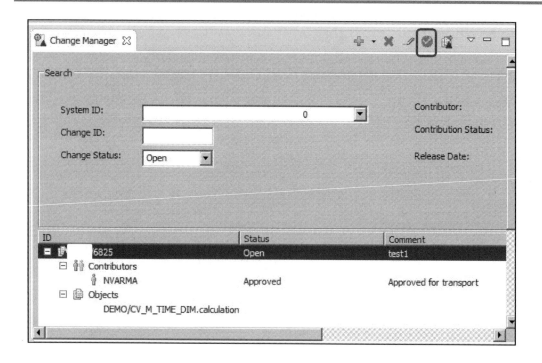

Change List will be released for transport. Subsequently the administrator can proceed to export the transport to target HANA system.

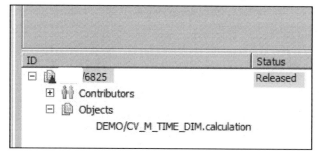

Made in the USA
Middletown, DE
02 August 2018